Defining Myself
Transmasculine Experience Through Poetry

Edited by:
Michael Eric Brown
Max Andeo Meyer

Published by
Boundless Endeavors, Inc.

Copyright © 2016
Michael Eric Brown and Max Andeo Meyer

Contributors: I.A. Avery, Shaun B., Isaac Oscar Bainbridge, Grayson Barnes, Michael Eric Brown, Will P. Craig, Al Cusack, Emrys Fevre, Tygh Lawrence-Clarke, Joshua Daniel Hunt, TJ Isaacs, Mitch Kellaway, Noah Mendez, Max Andeo Meyer, Para Modha, kaleb morrison, Casey O., Johnny W. Payne, Marval A Rex, S, Oliver Robertson, Noah S., Aaron Schmidt, Kai Schweizer, Liam J. Smietanski, Maverick Smith, Emrys Sparks, Dane Trotti, Char Utton, Jesse W., Joshua "Tygerwolfe" Ward, C. T. Whitley, Howie Wielandt, Dexter J Wiseman, Gavin Wyer, Caden Rocker, Owen Paul Karcher, Eugene SG Massey.

Cover Art Image by Felix J. Ross

All rights reserved. No part of this publication in paperback or e-book form may be reproduced, distributed, or transmitted in any form or by any means, including photocopying, recording, or other electronic or mechanical methods without the prior written permission of the author. For more information, please contact: publisher@boundlessendeavors.com

Rights to the individual works contained in this anthology are owned by the submitting authors and each has permitted the use of their work in this collection.

Printed in the United States of America

Published by Boundless Endeavors, Inc.
2250 NW 114th Place Unit 1P, PTY 21068
Miami, FL 33179
www.boundlessendeavors.com

First Printing, 2016

Library of Congress Control Number: 2016913570
ISBN-13: 978-0-9968309-4-2 (Print)
ISBN-10: 0-9968309-4-4 (Print)
ISBN-13: 978-0-9968309-5-9 (Ebook)
ISBN-10: 0-9968309-5-2 (Ebook)

CONTENTS

INTRODUCTION 1

SECTION I
Beginnings Pronouns Therapy Hormones Surgery 5

Becoming a Man 15
The Journey to Manhood 16
A Hexagram of Trans Tanka 18
She and Him 20
Pronoun Purgatory 22
One Word Can Change the World 23
Pronouns 24
Drop The S 27
I Don't Believe in Therapy 28
To The People Who Stare 29
Testosterone: My Liquid Courage 33
The Letter T 34
Late Night Voicemail 36
The Eyes of the World 37
Top Surgery 39
My two 40
Scars and Battle Wounds 41

SECTION II
Fears Anger Loss Dysphoria Discrimination 43

What Happens When 54
Sometimes We Rethink Things 55
Murderous Bathrooms 56

I Killed My Boyfriend's Girlfriend	57
Fear	58
A Brother Found	59
Midden	60
Perceptions	63
Wrong	67
Masculinity	70
Dialogue	71
Labels	73
Rival	75
Free	76
Sometimes…	78
Bird	79
Ice Cream Grief	80
Lost and Found	81
Still Here	83
My loss	84
Coming Home	85
An Open Letter to Little Girl	88
Deficit of Boyfriends	89
Belief is in the Mind of the Beholder	90
Inappropriate Questions	92
Troublemaker	94
A Eulogy For Dead Names	98
Dear Homophobia and Transphobia	101
Sometimes My Body is a Problem	103
Reflection	105
Many Years Ago	109

Untitled 110
The Sweater 111
Dysphoria 112

SECTION III
Changes Living Authentically Peace/Joy/Acceptance 113

The men 119
Matter 121
These Thighs 122
Geologic 124
Signposts 126
A Transgender Journey in Limerick Form 127
Show me 128
Masculinity on the Margins 129
Artwork 130
Stages 131
My Penis 132
The Taped and Tattered Man 134
True to me 136
The Catharsis Condition 139
Conglomeration of Genders 141
Am I sexy? 142
One Instant 144
Birthrite 145
Breakthrough 147
Haunted By Myself 149
Forthright 150

CONTRIBUTORS 151
REFERENCES 163

INTRODUCTION

We are Michael Eric Brown and Max Andeo Meyer—two guys who happen to be trans, and who have a passion for writing and a desire to reach others in the transmasculine community. What inspired us to publish this book, you ask? Just ask the individuals in this book how important they feel it is for their experiences to help others. We saw their need to reach a wide community, and a book seemed the most likely conduit for this to happen.

Many of us have sat down and penned (or typed) a few lines during the emotional stages of our journey—those deep, private thoughts that flow unrestricted to the surface sharing our pain, our anger, our fears, our excitement and joy. Those who have shared their work in this book have done so to help others in their gender exploration and journeys.

All are transmasculine, meaning they identify somewhere on the masculine side of the gender spectrum. Some may be fully transitioned female-to-male (FTM) while others may be non-binary, gender fluid or simply transmasculine, with or without having gone through a physical transition. It is not the physical that makes the person—it is the self-identification, the self-love and self-acceptance—and it is all these experiences in each of these individuals that help create our diverse community of transmasculine folks.

In this book, you will find the collective works of thirty-eight individuals who have revealed their deepest emotions in written word. Over seventy poems putting a voice to the process of living authentically in one's gender. Words which have come from the depths of their beings—from the ache of depression, the fiery pits of anger, darkness of their fears, and the deep wells of loss; as well as from their journeys of change to their passions of joy and acceptance.

We have divided the book into three sections, each with several themes and the poetry that portrays the experiences within those themes. These themes include: Beginnings, Pronouns, Therapy, Hormones, Surgery, Fears, Anger, Loss, Dysphoria, Discrimi-nation, Changes, Living Authentically, and Peace/Joy/Acceptance. These are just some of the experiences that transmasculine individuals encounter in their paths to living authentically in their self-identification and their gender expression. Each section has a brief few pages of introduction to the themes before the actual poetry begins. We have included these intros for those who may be just learning about transmasculine individuals to help clarify the importance and significance of these themes in our lives.

We thank everyone who submitted their works, and we are deeply sorry we were unable to include all the poetry that came in. We have kept this book with a rating equivalent to a PG-13, only because of a few instances of strong language. We agonized over whether to include a few poems that came in which had what could be considered "triggering" subject matter, such as rape and sexual abuse, and after much deliberation realized two things: 1) if we included "triggering" content, we would have to interrupt the flow of the sections with content warnings, and it could likely persuade some people not to read the book, perhaps worried they might run into a poem they are too emotionally vulnerable to handle; and 2) If we included those poems, we would have to rate the book as 18+, which potentially leaves out hundreds of individuals, especially since many of them are young teens still living at home, and the subject matter would be inappropriate.

Poets who have shared their experiences in this book:

I.A. Avery ❖ Shaun B. ❖ Isaac Oscar Bainbridge ❖ Grayson Barnes ❖ Michael Eric Brown ❖ Will P. Craig ❖ Al Cusack ❖ Emrys Fevre ❖ Tygh Lawrence-Clark ❖ Joshua Daniel Hunt ❖ TJ

Isaacs ❖ Mitch Kellaway ❖ Noah Mendez ❖ Max Andeo Meyer ❖ Para Modha ❖ kaleb morrison ❖ Casey O. ❖ Johnny W. Payne ❖ Marval A Rex ❖ S ❖ Oliver Robertson ❖ Noah S. ❖ Aaron Schmidt ❖ Kai Schweizer ❖ Liam J. Smietanski ❖ Maverick Smith ❖ Emrys Sparks ❖ Dane Trotti ❖ Char Utton ❖ Jesse W. ❖ Joshua "Tygerwolfe" Ward ❖ C. T. Whitley ❖ Howie Wielandt ❖ Dexter J Wiseman ❖ Gavin Wyer ❖ Caden Rocker ❖ Owen Paul Karcher ❖ Eugene SG Massey

We hope you enjoy this collection of transmasculine experience through poetry.

Michael Eric Brown
Max Andeo Meyer

SECTION I

Beginnings

Pronouns

Therapy

Hormones

Surgery

Beginnings

There are thousands of first times when a person transitions.

You will never forget the joy of hearing your chosen name for the first time or the first time introducing yourself, proclaiming your identity for the whole world to hear. Even better, the first time being introduced by another person, knowing someone else sees you as the person you always knew you were.

First time signing your new name will be monumental, making sure the curve of each letter fits you perfectly. You will start to write the old name the first few times.

Your first time shopping in the clothing section that matches your presentation, you will hesitantly approach the cash register, hoping the cashier will give you a ticket to a world you could never access. You will glow the first time you wear clothes that match your identity. This is followed by the first time looking in a mirror and not cringing and the first time smiling in a photograph.

If you medically transition, there will be the first time you see yourself in the mirror after they pull off the bandages and the first time you feel that needle pierce every layer of your skin. You will never want to stop talking after you hear your deepened voice for the first time. The first time shaving your face will be the last time you use the cheap razors.

You will try to not hyperventilate as you become hyper-conscious of the sound your urine makes against the toilet bowl the first time using the restroom matching your identity.

You will do your best to fit in the first time talking to cisgender men in an all-male space even if you don't approve of the occasional sexist jokes and conversations.

Your view of your transition will change the first time you experience your male privilege when a female classmate asks you to walk her to her dorm late at night because she is scared. You will experience shame from your privilege the first time you see a girl cross the street to avoid walking next to you at night.

The first time you explain your new identity to someone you love will change your life forever. There will be a last time you apologize for your existence. The first time you grieve for your old self will be easier than the first time you comfort someone who is grieving the loss of your old self.

The weight of disappointment from the first time you are misgendered after trying so hard to appear masculine will crush you if your goal is to appear masculine. The first time you defend your pronouns will be the last time you allow them to get away with misgendering you.

The first time a man picks a fight with you to prove your masculinity, you will wonder what price you are willing to pay to be accepted as masculine. You will never forget the first time you are bullied or discriminated against because you are a transman.

You will swear the heartache is worth it the first time someone tells you they love you just the way you are, that they only see you as how you present yourself.

Ultimately, there will be a first time feeling comfortable in your body and proud of your body when you realize you truly love yourself. This leads to your first time feeling confident in social situations, the first time you are respected and accepted as your true self, and the first time you feel like you belong in your body, your community, and your life story.

Nothing compares to the first time feeling alive.

Each first time marks a beginning: a new experience, a milestone, an opportunity, an accomplishment. Not every beginning stems from an ending and not every beginning has a first time. Sometimes when a person transitions the beginning is a continuation of their life with some minor adjustments, a new plot line in their life story. Some beginnings are filled with grief for lost family members and friends; while, other beginnings are filled with joy and excitement. Many beginnings are filled with fear for the future, and some beginnings take a lifetime to start.

It only takes a little self-acceptance for a new life to begin.

Pronouns

What is a pronoun? It is a word that refers to either the people talking (I, you) or someone that is being talked about (she, them, him). Contrary to public opinion, there are far more pronouns than just the ones most people use, which are generally binary words such as she, her, he and him. There are, however, several other gender-neutral terms that some people choose to use, also. Gender neutral pronouns are those which do not associate a gender with the individual who is being discussed. Some of these include; they, them, theirs (which can be used in the singular), and others such as ze (pronounced "zee") and hir (pronounced "here"). There are other people who don't want to be referred to with any pronoun, but want only their name to be used.

Think about pronouns for a moment. If you were born male, and you feel your gender identity is male or masculine – you're generally referred to as he, him, his, or sir, right? Imagine if everyone started calling you she, miss, her and even if you correct them, they continue. Would you be angry? Sure you would. They would be disrespecting you if they called you a traditionally female pronoun. If it continued day after day, week after week, month after month, and no amount of correcting does any good, the anger stage would be superseded by a depression, knowing you were stuck in a place that was defined by other people, and you had no control.

When a trans or gender non-conforming person is referred to with a pronoun that doesn't match how they see themselves, it can make them feel disrespected, invalidated, dismissed, alienated, or dysphoric. Some may appear physically as a female, but they feel more masculine, and vice versa. Some don't see themselves as masculine or feminine, but instead somewhere in between. Using the wrong pronoun for someone can be a source of frustration to the trans and genderqueer/gender non-conforming communities.

Gender is a choice, not a given, and there is not so much of a distinction between male and female, but rather, it is a spectrum of identities. Some people's gender identity is non-binary, and using conventional pronouns are, in effect, assigning them a binary identity. The physical body doesn't determine one's gender, because a body is just a sex. A well-known saying about gender came from Virginia Prince (1971), when she said "Any kind of carving that you might do on me might change my sex, but it would not change my gender, because *my gender, my self-identity, is between my ears, not between my legs*" (emphasis added).

Asking and correctly using someone's personal pronoun is one of the most basic ways to show your respect for their gender identity.

Therapy

For some people, images of lying on a couch in a shrink's office gives way to joking and shaming those who admit they are seeing someone. For others, regular visits to a counselor or therapist is a part of their lives despite what others think. Major life events, such as losing a job, a home, a spouse through divorce, or a close friend or family member's death, is often the catalyst for choosing to seek help. For others, life itself with its unfairness and seemingly never-ending bad luck is the push to find ways of coping with it all.

For many trans people, it might be the confusion they are experiencing on a daily basis, trying to fit in a mold they aren't comfortable with. Many are shamed and ridiculed by others for trying to be themselves, and face harassment and bullying while growing up; then they find it even worse when they begin to live in their authentic and true genders. They face losing their families and their jobs, and they have to cope with making decisions like which bathroom to use, or even whether or not take the risk of going out in public wondering if this might be the day they are beaten or killed.

Those on the more masculine side of the gender spectrum many times grow up feeling anger from being forced into a feminine role in society, having to cope with the sexism and misogyny that comes with being perceived as female. They fight everyone and everything to simply be themselves, and they begin to think about beginning to take testosterone and having chest reconstruction surgery.

Therapy for a gender transition is a highly suggested and often-times needed course of action for making the life decision of medically altering one's body to be more in line with how they feel inside. Therapy is oftentimes a vital part of the process, and this statement isn't limited to just following the suggested guidelines on the path to obtaining hormones or surgery.

We need to take a look at the places we've each come from – those places of discomfort and stress. So many transgender people jump into the transition process thinking ahead of time that living as their affirmed gender will be the answer to their problems, and they can be themselves, and everything will be happiness and roses from that point forward. They somehow equate "transition" as the "cure" (Brown, 2015).

Transition is not the cure, and it will not fix everything. A positive attitude, ability to accept life on its terms and rise above the negativity, and the capacity to embrace positivity in all situations—that is what you can learn from therapy and how to succeed in life.

Learning skills to cope with one's life is what therapy is all about. Learning to look within one's self and being able to be honest about how we feel, finding out why we feel this way, and how we can feel differently. Learning how to cope with the negativity that surrounds us, and how to effectively communicate our needs and our wants. Learning to control the anger, or get past the shame. Learning to take care of one's self in the best possible way in order to have a future filled with inner happiness and contentment rather than all those negative emotions we have come to accept as somehow inescapable.

Life is not always perfect. But it's all we've got, and it is up to us to make it the best life we can. Sometimes having some professional guidance along the way can make the difference between a life of continuing misery or a life of contentment and happiness.

Hormones

Some transmasculine individuals receive testosterone as a form of hormone replacement therapy to masculinize their bodies by deepening their voices, creating facial and body hair, shifting their body weight, stopping menses, and increasing their muscle mass.

These changes can increase a person's confidence and self-acceptance as one form of gender confirming treatment. According to the Gay and Lesbian Alliance Against Defamation, 78 percent of the trans people surveyed experienced "improved psychological functioning after receiving gender confirming treatment" (2013).

Depending on where a person lives, it can be a struggle for transmasculine individuals to access this treatment. There may be no doctors in the area willing to work with transmasculine individuals or doctors who are knowledgeable in testosterone treatment. According to a survey conducted by the National Center for Transgender Equality and the National Gay and Lesbian Task Force (2010), 19 percent of the transmasculine individuals surveyed were refused health care based on their transgender status, and only 66 percent of transmasculine individuals who wanted testosterone had accessed it. An additional 61 percent of the transmasculine people surveyed reported having to teach their doctors about transgender health care.

Depending on the healthcare provider, transmasculine individuals might need to receive counseling and letters from a psychiatrist before the healthcare provider will offer them a prescription. Some doctors make their patients sign and agree to the side effects testosterone will cause and agree to the fact that the consequences of long-term testosterone use are still unknown and largely under researched. Other doctors require transmasculine individuals to be formally diagnosed with gender dysphoria. Not all transgender individuals suffer from gender dysphoria. Non-binary individuals struggle even more to get a testosterone prescription.

Even if a person manages to find a doctor who is willing and knowledgeable to provide testosterone, that does not mean that the doctor or the testosterone prescription itself are covered by the individual's health insurance. According to the National Center for Transgender Equality (2016), only 17 states have policies banning health insurance discrimination towards transgender people. Of those 17 states, only 11 states have nondiscrimination policies which apply to private and public insurance companies. The out-of-pocket costs of hormone replacement treatment can prohibit people from obtaining the treatment they need and deserve.

Once an individual has a testosterone prescription, they must adhere to pharmaceutical laws which can make picking up their prescription inconvenient. As a controlled substance, traveling domestically and abroad with testosterone can be challenging or impossible.

When a transmasculine individual has a testosterone bottle in his hand, it can seem like that oil is made of pure gold. After all of the struggles to obtain it, the pain of the needle or the inconveniences of the gel appear to be minor discomforts. The first dose is a terrifying yet exhilarating step towards a body that fits. The changes are slow at first, but each change is noticed and checked off of a list of puberty milestones. In the end, it is thrilling to see yourself in the mirror as you have imagined yourself to look and comforting to hear your voice as you know it should sound.

Surgery

Not every transmasculine individual chooses to have surgery as part of the transition process. Having gender reassignment surgery is a personal choice, and there are many reasons why some don't pursue this option. One reason for not pursuing it is the costs involved, but also health and personal reasons are common reasons also.

There are three types of surgeries that are available to transmasculine individuals; chest reconstruction surgery (also known as "top" surgery, hysterectomy), removal of the uterus, and if ovaries are removed also, it is known as an oophorectomy), and genital reconstruction surgery (also known as "bottom" surgery).

Due to dysphoria, as well as the uncomfortable process of binding to hide one's anatomy, many elect to have top surgery. This involves removal of breast tissue, and nipple grafts or resizing/repositioning of nipples, areola or both. This may be the only surgery some individuals choose to have done. With the effects of testosterone creating the secondary sex characteristics such as facial and body hair, redistribution of body fat, squaring of the jaw, deepening of the voice, it is essential to many transmasculine individuals to have top surgery in order to relieve dysphoria, and to have the appearance of a male chest.

The other surgeries are a matter of personal choice, as well as whether or not they are covered by insurance, which in all likelihood, they are not. For most, insurance coverage has not been an option, and the various surgeries can range from several thousand dollars up to over one hundred thousand dollars each. As far as which type of bottom surgery, transmasculine individuals have a choice, neither of which is optimal.

One surgery, the metoidioplasty, creates a micro penis, with or without implanted testicles and with or without the ability to urinate through the new penis. The constructed penis, created from the tissues in the genital area, is the more common choice due to costs. The other surgery is a phalloplasty, which involves constructing a penis from donor skin from other areas of the body (abdomen, groin/leg, forearm, and/or side of the upper torso) and grafted onto the pubic area. Usually the urethra is extended so one can urinate through the penis, and erections are achieved with either a permanent or temporary rod, or an implanted pump device. This procedure is generally done in several stages with multiple surgeries over a period of months up to a couple of years.

Surgery is a personal choice in one's gender exploration and journey. Some people start out thinking they will not have any surgeries. Then they change their mind once taking testosterone. Others know from the start that surgery is their goal. There is no right or wrong decision when it comes to surgery, and someone who chooses not to undergo any surgical procedure may still identify completely or partially as a man or somewhere along the masculine side of center on the gender spectrum.

⌘ ⌘ ⌘ ⌘ ⌘

Becoming a Man
Gavin Wyer
2011

This day I am a man

Not through body altered

Or magic drug injected

But quiet introspection

Of whom I've always been

Careful thought provoked

Speaks to my interior

A new way of being

Identifies my truth

I toss the broken armour

And gain a sacred strength

Recognising my brothers

And my place among them

The Journey to Manhood
Joshua Daniel Hunt
2014

You have what I covet.

The pristine, functioning, magical, mystical male physique.

I want my puzzled reality to finally be set.

Striving to obtain the goal,

ever thinking and toiling.

It possesses me in my darkest, deepest soul.

To be whole and complete.

WaitingPrayingSchemingCryingPushingYelling
ShovingWailing.

Disgruntled, I play in my back yard; surmising I've been cheated.

You have what I need.

An intricate puzzle being built

one

slow

painstaking…piece at a time.

Forming a DaVinci that only I can adore and conceive of.

Immaculate creation.

I have what I was given;

choices.

And the breathtaking gift of life.

This body betrayed me and brought me nothing
but mind-numbing strife.
Choices.
Life itself revolves around and is entangled like gnarled
    vines by them.
They dance
and sing
and whirl
around in your mind.
Sometimes it stops, and
holds still.
You listen.
And you realize a 'choice' wasn't yours to find.
In the blanketing silence emerges
my destiny.
Who I am. What I am.
I wake.
Thank God finally I wake with a SLAM.
No need to covet or shout.
The final piece has been placed.
Ah—-Joshua.
How could there have been any doubt?

A Hexagram of Trans Tanka
Marval A Rex
2016

Un-nameable Me

The lamp lit faces
Bright discs confused by beauty
Un-nameable me

Strange Music

My pink palette tastes
The acrid sweat of time lost
Singing sweet other's songs

Church Soliloquy

Found, under the stairs
An old building leaking light
A young girl; a boy

Masked Line

I took off my mask
Beneath it was true new flesh
Jagged and novel

Careful Drowning

Below each fountain
Our bodies are the structure
Tending your sharp coins

Spoken Transitions

Echoed traditions
The words change before all eyes
Once she, they, he, me

She and Him
S
2016

In dreams did He rise,
formed from a longing.
Something felt amiss.
She did not know why.
Why there was longing,
for things that were
for the boys,
for parts that were
attributed to men.

When He came,
She was not sure from where.
In play did He arrive,
a game of house
where she played the other role.
And somehow it felt right.

She began to think more about Him.
A new imaginary friend to play as.
It made sense.

Slowly He crept into Her mind more,

More decisions made as Him.
"Should I wear that shirt? No, He would feel restricted."
"Should I do that thing? No, that brings on the
    discomfort."

Until things began to make less sense again.
Was this body of Hers or was this body of His?
Neither able to exist in harmony.

Some things are a delicate dance,
each night where dreams were of Him trying to exist,
Dreams where She tried to make sense how to exist.

She and Him,
trying to work it out.
It was Them.
That was harmony.

They worked together to exist.

In reality They exist,
Both.
She and Him.

Pronoun Purgatory
Dexter J Wiseman
2016

I get called she, her, madam, miss
My throat goes tight, I feel quite sick
I bind my chest and pack my pants
I cut my hair, with hope perchance…
that you will see me as I am.
He, him, chap, mate, Mr, sir,
even "Oi, you" I'd take over "her."
I know I don't pass yet, but give me a break.
I do what I can, not pretending or fake
Just living my truth, working out my life plan
To get through this world as a proud trans MAN!

One Word Can Change the World
Noah S.
2016

The word *she* is a knife.

It slices me and dismembers me to the point of no return.

The word *she* is a gun.

You pull the trigger and watch me burn.

The word *she* eats me up.

And soon there is nothing left of me.

The remains of what I was is longer there to see.

The word *he* is a pillow.

It catches my head as I lay to rest.

The word *he* is a bowl of chocolate pudding.

It melts in my mouth and makes me feel the best.

The word *he* is my salvation.

It embraces me with warmth like no other.

It fills me with the happiness that I need to rediscover.

Pronouns
Isaac Oscar Bainbridge
2016

Imagine, you just bought a new summer dress.

You feel confident

and you look amazing,

but someone comes up to you and says

"Sir...Can you direct me to the nearest train station?"

You stare at them blankly, and then reply

"That way"

and walk away.

Imagine, you just bought a new suit and tie.

You feel confident

and you look amazing,

but the store clerk counts your change and says

"Miss...Is that all you'll be buying today?"

You stare at them blankly, and then reply

"That's all"

and walk away.

Now, imagine,

every "she," "her," "miss"

is another slice along his cold, scared skin

and nothing has changed,
apart from his name,
and they refuse to use that too.

So, why do pronouns matter to Trans* people?
Whether it be "she," "him," "them"
these small words are a key part to an expression and an identity
that must be shown to be yourself.
Not recognizable by clothes or hairstyles,
being trans runs deeper than that.
It flows through your veins
and takes over your brain
until you can be the person you were meant to be.

Now, imagine
every "he," "him," "sir"
is another slice along her cold scared skin
and nothing has changed,
apart from her name,
and they refuse to use that too.

So, don't tell me
"It's okay because I knew you before."
Don't ask me
"Is it okay if I call you it?"

Don't tell me I'm wrong,
You're wrong.
Don't tell me
"But you were born a girl."
Don't ask me
"Aren't you too young to know?"
No!
Just use the right word.
They will use the right word.
I promise.

Drop The S
Joshua "Tygerwolfe" Ward
2016

Drop the "S"
That is not me.
That "S" represents everything
I don't want to be.

The "S" is in "dresses,"
In "dolls" and in "styles."
It's the "S" that depresses,
That confines and riles.

Drop the "S,"
Leave it behind.
One letter can make,
People so blind.

One little letter,
So simple and small.
Such a strange thing,
To matter at all.

Drop that "S", now,
Why can't you see?
It's wrong – I'll tell you how:
I am simply "He."

I Don't Believe in Therapy
Noah Mendez
2016

give me the name of your
first unborn child let me
chew on it and spit out your
daddy issues and fetishes
never fully sane just
Girl Who Thinks They Are Boy
Girl Who Has Been To Psych Ward
Girl Who Is Unreliable Witness

here pop one two three five pills
write me a dissertation on the
first time you kissed a girl and if
it made you grow a beard or something
lie down on my couch and tell me how
wearing boxers gets you high
let out all your freak I
am certified and here to tell you
I am authority figure and
you are crazy

To The People Who Stare
Howie Wielandt
2016

To the people who stare,
No, I'm not a girl.
No, I'm not gay.
These are not boobs,
This is my chest.
I'm a man.

You want to know what's in my pants?
Well you'll have to take me out to dinner first.
Yes boys have long hair,
I'm cutting it this weekend, Not to worry.
Again, no, I'm not a lesbian.
Ever heard of transgender?

Well that's me, gender bender over here, breaking every rule.
Maybe I should wear a shirt explaining who I am.

To the people who stare, as if I'm in this store standing in my
 underwear:
Take a picture it'll last longer.
All I wanted was this can of soup, and yet I find you staring, and
 your child tugging on your sleeve asking "Is that a boy or a
 girl?"

Haven't you ever been told "it's impolite to stare."
Allow me to repeat myself: I. Am. Not. A. Girl.
I am also not, she, it, that, thing, or tranny.
I am a person,
Who also happens to be transitioning from female to male.

So you say I chose this way?
Wake up, Quick, Gun to your head, Pick your poison:

A lack of breath or dysphoria so bad you feel as if you're going to
    crawl out of your own skin.

Slow shallow breaths while you panic,
Worried someone will figure it out when you take a piss.
We become hashtags,
Mourning our family members, and fighting for those who
    couldn't fight anymore.
#IJustWantToPee! #HisNameWasBrandon!
    #HerNameWasLeelah #OrlandoShooting!
This is what we've become.

It was Charles Bukowski who said,
"Some suicides are never recorded."
We walk in spaces that aren't safe for us,
We're afraid to ask for help,
We're afraid for our lives.
That fear breeds a war zone for an already neglected system.

Log online and find "another one."
We become "those people" to the media.
Our private lives exposed,
Every infraction examined.
That is, When we're actually counted as people.
Even then, we're misrepresented, our identities erased as if
    being trans doesn't exist.

And god forbid we get killed while working in sex work,
I can see the headline now: "A man wearing a dress was killed."
Like it's somehow our fault.
Like being trans is a contagious disease that causes people to
    take the life of another.
I'll tell you what the disease is,
It's hate that's been bred from ignorance, and misconceptions.

Open your mouth,
And you out yourself,

But how can I be quiet,
When all around me is hate,
Yelling at me,
Telling me what I'm doing is wrong,
That who I am,
Is wrong,
How can I stay silent?

I feel like I'm serving a prison sentence, that one day I'll be free,
The days start slow and painful and become, slow and comfortable.

So to the people who stare,
My transition is not a choice,
Do you think I like choosing between the happiness of my parents or my own mental health?
Do you think I enjoy staying up until 3am,
Lying awake in my bed, Pissed off at the world,
Stuck on a roller coaster I can't get off of?

My mother,
She means well,
"Have faith" she says, But how can I have faith in something that constantly works against me?

My father,
He doesn't understand,
"I was raised in that era" he says, But how can you say the things you do knowing you have me for a kid.

My brother,
Fourteen years old, confused in a game of tug of war.
"The kids at school talk about you and make jokes" he says,
He's starting high school next year, a place where he can get a fresh start.

Both of them,

I feel guilty,
I've replaced their first born daughter, I've given them two sons,
Something they weren't prepared for.

For parents who are unaccepting of their LGBT+ child, hug them tightly and learn to accept them because one day it might be too late.

I'm always waiting,
Waiting to come out, Waiting to be accepted, Waiting for hormones, Waiting for surgeries,
Having a staredown with a clock,
Frustrated because time is like sand, Slipping through my fingers,
I don't want to wait anymore,
I want to live my life with my body whole,
I don't want to hide parts,
I want to show it off,

I'll be proud of my scars,
All of them.

Me,
In my dreams,
I have goals,
To sit in the sun,
My chest bare,
Without a care,
In the world.
My transition will come to an end,
And I'll finally be able to breathe,
In my own skin.

So to the people who stare,
Do you understand yet?

Testosterone: My Liquid Courage
Caden Rocker
2009

My liquid courage cannot be bought in a liquor store.

My liquid courage requires a prescription.

My liquid courage cannot be swallowed.

My liquid courage is injected with a needle plunged into my thigh.

My liquid courage does not leave me with a hangover.

My liquid courage helps me be me.

The Letter T
Michael Eric Brown
2000

T is for the Twisting of my emotions
when people look at me and
they see someone different than I see,
a face and a body
that betray me.
They don't see the man inside,
crying to get out and be seen.
But I know the beginning of a new life
begins with the letter T.

T is for the Teacher
who uses my birth name,
calls me a she, and
refuses to let me use
my preferred name.
Because I don't look like the man inside,
I'm crying to get out and be seen.
And I know the beginning of a new life
begins with the letter T.

T is for the Trouble
with binary gender,

when people can only see
male and female
based on appearance.
I don't look like the man inside,
I'm ready to get out and be seen.
And I know the beginning of my new life
Begins with the letter T.

T is for Testosterone,
the giver of maleness,
the inner truth brought out
to be seen by others
and not just by me.
I will look like the man inside, and
I am getting out, I want to be seen.
I know the beginning of my new life
Begins with the letter T.

Late Night Voicemail
kaleb morrison
2016

medical intervention
SRS FTM
not a ceremony not a ritual
searching within this system leaves me lost
no context no story

I am buried in questions fighting to do "the right thing"
make the right choice
to do good to be whole.

I do not know my body though
I don't know if I can go through with it and I see no
    avenue to answers

I have felt like a boy for my whole life
I didn't eat when I was a teenager because I didn't want
    curves or breasts
I wanted to be hard and strong
I wanted to be clean and free
I wanted to be raw and exposed
I did not and do not feel like a woman and I don't know
    why this is

I want wholeness I want connection I want realness.
now I don't know who I am because I am fighting so hard
introspecting so hard
I want me back I want my heart back

all I can do is call and cancel and sit in the questions
comforted only by a wisp of honesty
and a scrap of courage

The Eyes of the World
Joshua Daniel Hunt
2015

I've been marked.

Languidly and deliberately marked.

Sweat breaks and beads from every pore.

When will the eyes upon my shame

and loathing be consumed?

When will this growth be obliterated

and slammed into the dross where it

should have always resided?

A Sharpie glides upon my skin and is my mark

of subjugation and freedom.

The eyes that look upon me are equally a

distortion and the truth.

The lights are blaring as I climb upon the pristine, white, sterile

surface to my authenticity.

Hands washing.

Masks on.

Technical movements that form a well-known dance.

A typical day for my liberators.

I inhale deeply, so as to fill my

soul with that indistinct odor.

Count to...

Sir?

Sir?

Sir?

Yes,

I am here!

The eyes that look upon me adjust and glimmer

with sincerity.

The mark is gone.

I smile,

and, for once, slip peacefully

into an untroubled slumber.

Top Surgery
Liam J. Smietanski
2015

"Good bye" to an unfamiliar reflection in the mirror.

He lay down; the doctor stood over him, "Count back from 10."

"10, 9 …"

Later, he opens his eyes much relieved as to the mirror he turns and there is his reflection, "I'm so glad to see you!"

Nurse walks in, "How's the pain?"

"Gone!"

My two
Mitch Kellaway
2013

i.
couple kelloid half moons
pectoral rims i'm told
they beg concealment
angry pink & jag ged
revealing too much to knowing lookers
of my (body) history—
that i took
what parts i needed & shed the rest
abandoning tissue like a sculptor's excess
stone

ii.
slashes— my two
won't don't portend
injury nor disease
too unrandom for an accident
a symmetry too crafted
cannot will not be residue of emergency
look! away / closer
they lie emblazoned
but never whisper come probe
my wired flesh
my wounds warmed over
my made-to-clash my
subterranean

Endnote: "Look!" inspired by Jamison Green, "'Look! No Don't!' The Visibility Dilemma for Transsexual Men" in Kate More and Stephen Whittle (eds), *Reclaiming Genders: Transsexual Grammars at the Fin de Siecle,* (New York: Cassell, 1999).

Scars and Battle Wounds
Caden Rocker
2016

This Journey comes with its own set of battle wounds and scars.
There are the physical scars from surgery and the emotional battle wounds that may not be visible.
The abscess from relationships lost or changed drastically, never to be the same.
The multiple puncture wounds from the ignorant and fear-fueled hate speech that pierces you to your core like a freshly sharpened dagger.
The process of "coming out" as Trans can be like constantly walking through a minefield, walking your Truth can sometimes end in an explosion.
Even those who "mean well" can leave you with your fair share of cuts, scrapes, bumps, bruises, and maybe even a few broken bones.
I will not hide any of my scars.
I will now proudly go shirtless exposing my scars from top surgery to their first summer sunshine.
The scars on my now breastless chest will always remind me of how hard and how far I have come in my fight, my war to be able to live my life as my authentic self.
My scars and wounds may have come with pain but I refuse to suffer or avoid living the life I want, deserve, and have earned.

⌘ ⌘ ⌘ ⌘ ⌘

SECTION II

Fears

Anger

Loss

Dysphoria

Discrimination

Fears

Nothing is scarier than making a monumental change in one's life. Transition affects every aspect of a person's life from the socks they wear to something as pivotal as a person's name. Many new doors are opened while old ways of life are abandoned entirely. For transmasculine people, day-to-day life is an adventure. The most trivial acts like using a public restroom or going to the department of motor vehicles can be a perilous journey filled with discrimination, bullying, and the threat of physical violence.

Some transmasculine people worry about the man they will become: who will they be? What will they look like? Where will they fit in society? How will loved ones react to the news that the girl they knew died to expose a man they never knew existed? Transmasculine people question whether they will be accepted in male spaces; whether their lives will feel happy and complete; whether they will like the changes testosterone makes on their bodies; whether they will be accepted by friends, family members, potential employers, and possible mates; whether they will be respected as the men they know they are; whether they will be able to withstand the pain of the needles and scalpels; whether they will pass as men when it matters most for their safety and acceptance in society; whether they will ever be able to accept themselves; and whether that love will ever be reciprocated.

Anxiety can erode a person from the inside out, especially when every part of a person's life becomes unpredictable. This anxiety can lead to depression and suicidal thoughts. When a person questions every aspect of their life, it can cause them to question the value of their existence. According to a study conducted by the National Center for the Transgender Equality and the National Gay and Lesbian Task Force (Grant, Mottett, & Tanis, 2010), 41 percent of the transpeople surveyed had attempted suicide compared to 1.6 percent in the general population.

When a transmasculine person begins transition, he cannot know whether he is headed towards a better life. He only knows that he is making himself more comfortable in this moment. By starting to transition, he starts the terrifying process of telling the truth. He must tell the truth to family members, to friends, to doctors, to judges, and to himself. For better or worse, he must face his fears, claim his right to exist as the person he knows he is, and defend his identity as he has defined it.

Loss

Loss is a common theme in life—from losing our toys to our first tooth; to losing friends to trust; to losing our virginity or innocence; to losing a game or losing a job promotion; or losing a loved one to a battle with illness to going through a painful divorce or losing a pet.

Sometimes unexpected, sometimes a choice, and other times a relief - loss is an emotional inevitability for all life on the planet. The prospect of loss is oftentimes so scary we try to prevent it from happening, often at the expense of making ourselves miserable during the time preceding the loss. Then there are those who look forward to a loss, anticipating a time of freedom from something or someone that has been holding them back, or thinking that somehow that loss will enable them to finally be happy. There are no right or wrong perspectives or feelings when it comes to loss. There is only facing it head-on and moving through the various emotions one will experience until we get to the other side. That other side might be better, or worse, or merely different.

For those individuals who are facing a decision on whether to pursue a physical gender transition, the aspect of loss is one of the more prominent considerations. Being born with a female-appearing body, and having been told how to dress, what to say, and even how to think and behave as a female can go against every fiber of one's being if they don't identify as female. They suffer through the social nuances of female expectations, and many times live with the fear of abuse, rape, sexism, and the oppression that is common for the female half of society.

When these individuals finally get to a place where they not only acknowledge they aren't female, but are ready to go through the process of physically changing their appearance to match their authentic identity, they are often faced with three kinds of losses:

One is the "good" type of loss - the loss of a life of being misgendered, a life full of societal expectations of females, a life which has been repressed and even oppressed, and for many, even the surgery to help them become more masculine appearing means losing the body that has long defied them.

Another type of loss many of these people face are the hard ones - losing family, friends, jobs and housing. There is evidence of this in the statistics, with a large percentage of transgender individuals experiencing family rejection, many losing their apartments due to discrimination, even being denied adequate health care and losing their jobs because of transition. The losses are staggering and all too common.

There is also one other loss that some people who transition don't think about ahead of time, and it can present itself just when things are going well – when they are seen in their affirmed gender, they are happy with how they look and feel, and life seems to be going in a positive direction. Something unexpected will come along, sometimes quietly and slowly creeping up on them, and at other times it's a sudden realization – the loss of their former self. For some people, it is a grieving process. They might be thinking of all the years they lost before transition, or they might realize that they no longer can be active in a certain group or community, such as frequenting women-only spaces. Still others realize something they had prior to transition but no longer have now – maybe the ability to "ooh" and "aah" over a toddler in public (because now they are a strange man), or the loss of someone offering to change a car tire, since as a man, we should be able to do it ourselves.

Transitioning to one's affirmed gender is a journey, and for most on the transmasculine spectrum, it evolves without too many issues. But, for many, there is the experience of losing various facets of our lives in the process. Would we change our minds, or wish we hadn't transitioned? The greater majority acknowledge the risks and the potential losses and accept that in order to live authentically, the losses are a sad, but inevitable part of the journey.

Anger

Anger. Just the word itself brings up uncomfortable feelings in some of us. It is an emotion that very few people enjoy, and one that manifests itself in a multitude of behaviors. It can be individual or a group shared emotion, and can be unfounded, well-founded, or even a righteous anger.

Anger is completely normal, and many times healthy emotion. But it can also be corrosive, and can be harmful to one's physical and mental health if not dealt with constructively. For transmasculine individuals, this anger can start growing and cultivating from a very young age, continuing to fester until it explodes or otherwise presents itself in various harmful behaviors.

When a child enters the world, it is assigned a sex—male or female. Through the next several years, they are given a myriad of social cues that are meant to reinforce this assignment. At some point, a transgender child begins to feel uncomfortable with some of these social expectations. They may not be able to put it into words what they feel, except that they know what they are taught to feel, or do, or how to dress, or what toys they can play with—they just know it isn't right for them. In the ideal situation, which does on occasion exist, parents will take the time to listen to their child, and realize the problem might be related to a gender and assigned sex mismatch. In most cases, however, the child grows up knowing they don't "fit in" to the social expectations put on them.

For those who are assigned female at birth but whose gender identities don't fit the "mold" of "female," they find themselves at odds with nearly everything they encounter: The constant barrage of girls' toys, being forced to wear dresses, or being prevented from playing on the boys' sport teams. Later, as they mature, they are taught not to sleep around, yet their male friends brag about their conquests, they experience an onslaught of sexist remarks and behaviors, and they learn to walk in pairs or they become a target. They pursue employment only to find they aren't paid as much as their male co-workers, people don't listen to them and treat them like they don't know what they are talking about.

It is understandable then, how transmasculine individuals can become angry. The anger can start as early as two or three years old, or it may start when they hit puberty and their secondary sex characteristics begin to develop. At some point, their parents made them start wearing a shirt, rather than running around topless like the other boys. Then they discover they have to wear bras, and they are confronted with this thing called menstruation.

The anger may be insidious, lurking quietly through the years, sometimes presenting itself through depression, or self-harm. For others, it may surface on a regular basis, creating havoc with family, friends, and employers. Many of these individuals don't even realize what their anger is all about, or where it comes from. They only know they have this emotion and they fight for their right to be themselves in every situation.

Sometimes, the anger turns into shame or guilt. Other times, depression takes over. At times, the anger is directed inward, and we are angry at the body that betrays us, while for others the anger is at others—for the discriminatory remarks and behaviors towards us because we don't conform to their ideas of gender binary. Sometimes it's directed at the system—the bureaucracy that makes it difficult and expensive to not only have proper medical help, but even to change our ID to reflect our preferred names and gender.

Anger is a common theme among transmasculine individuals who are either early in their physical transition or for those who have chosen not to pursue medical treatment. In most cases, it is understandable and necessary in order for them to survive the trauma of being perceived and treated as a female when they know they are not. Learning how to effectively manage the anger and constructively turn it into something positive is really the only true path to healing from the pain that triggered the anger to begin with.

Dysphoria

Imagine waking up and feeling so self-conscious about your appearance that you couldn't leave your bed. Imagine knowing you are masculine but everyone insists you are a beautiful woman. Imagine believing you are so ugly that you are undeserving of love. Imagine acting every day, pretending to be the person your loved ones and society want you to be. Imagine despising a part of your body so fiercely that you try to perform surgery on yourself in a drunken rage. Imagine everyone you met refused to acknowledge your existence and belittled you by using the wrong pronouns. Imagine feeling so uncomfortable in your body that you try to physically crawl out of your skin. Imagine knowing something was wrong with your body, screaming that it was physically hurting you, and being ignored by medical professionals. Imagine feeling so disconnected from your body that you can only watch it walk through your life from above as you haunt yourself like a ghost, not caring if your body were healthy or sick, dead or alive.

That is what it is like to live with gender dysphoria.

The Canadian Psychological Association defines gender dysphoria as "the unhappiness some people feel about their physical sex and/or gender role" (Cohen & Anderson, 2014). It is the disconnect between the sex assigned at birth and gender identity.

Dysphoria can cause depression and anxiety. These feelings can be alleviated by gender confirming actions like hormone replacement therapy, a name and pronouns which match the perceived gender identity, presenting as the perceived gender identity, and gender confirmation surgery. If you know someone who is suffering from gender dysphoria, you can help them by validating their existence, showing compassion and respect, and engaging the person in distracting activities.

Not all transmasculine individuals experience dysphoria. Likewise, dysphoria affects people in different ways. The negative feelings may not be as severe for some individuals. Regardless, evidence of persistent gender dysphoria and a diagnosis of gender identity disorder by a mental health professional is required by many doctors for them to prescribe testosterone or refer a person for surgery and is required by many judges for them to allow someone to change their legal gender.

Some people want to do away with the term "gender dysphoria" altogether since it infers that gender nonconforming individuals are mentally ill and must be cured. It also creates more obstacles for people who do not experience gender dysphoria and who still need to change their legal documents and receive hormone replacement therapy.

Discrimination

Transgender people are often seen by others as non-conforming to a natural or inherited identity, so they are stigmatized, and often victims of social bias, harassment, bullying, and even violence. Trans and gender non-conforming people face discrimination in virtually every aspect of social life. . The statistics of discrimination and its effects on the trans community have been widely published, and are indisputable evidence to the severity.

Levels of discrimination can range from purposefully misgendering, being passed over for a promotion, being fired from a job, being evicted, or being forced to use the wrong restroom; to verbal harassment, being spat on, being bullied, sexual assault, violence and even murder. In some countries, it is illegal to be transgender, with negative consequences if discovered, including imprisonment or death. Media helps to perpetuate discrimination, by influencing people's opinions, identities, choices and lives.

A landmark survey has revealed reeling statistics on trans discrimination; 53 percent of those surveyed had been verbally harassed or disrespected in a public place, while 90 percent experienced harassment, mistreatment or discrimination on the job. Physical assault was reported at 61 percent and sexual assault 64 percent. Youth in grades K-12 were harassed at the rate of 78 percent, 35 percent of this age group experienced physical assault, and 12 percent were victims of sexual assault.

Due to discrimination, "A staggering 41% of respondents reported attempting suicide compared to 1.6% of the general population, with rates rising for those who lost a job due to bias (55%), were harassed/bullied in school (51%), had low household income, or were the victim of physical assault (61%) or sexual assault (64%)" (Grant, et al. 2010). 41 percent of the trans people attempting suicide have been victims of forced sex or rape (Clements-Nolle, Marx and Katz 2006, 59).

Trans people are disproportionately affected by hate violence in our communities. Culturally, there are significant divisions in how individuals from different political parties, geographical locations, and religious affiliations perceive and, therefore, behave towards transgender people. On account of societal perceptions, laws, and continuing discrimination, trans people lose jobs, homes, families, friends and more.

For transmasculine individuals who have not yet physically transitioned, societal lack of understanding, perception, and treatment increased discrimination towards these individuals occurs due to the difficulty of recognizing these individuals as masculine. They are purposely misgendered by family, peers, and employers. Their male names and pronouns are not respected. They are forced to conform to society's expectation of using a female restroom, and they can be harassed or experience violence due to their appearance.

In the United States, there are several areas in our lives that are illegal to discriminate against, such as: age, disability, genetic information, race/color, religion, sex and more. Gender is not in this list, except in a limited capacity in certain states or jurisdictions. It is essential that advocates and activists continue to make progress in legislation and continue to educate because it is imperative that transgender individuals be treated and seen as equals in society.

⌘⌘⌘⌘⌘

What Happens When
Owen Paul Karcher
2016

Movement.
Spaces expanded. Attention turned.
Towards masculinity. Away from feminine
The terror my body now causes
and the tremble in my heart
as I fear what happens when,
and if, they find out my genitals
still look like the ones they label
inferior, conquerable, less powerful.
The ones that birth us all.

Sometimes We Rethink Things
Shaun B.
2015

I wish I may I wish I might

Find a better star tonight

For mine is not so bright

Darkness overwhelms the light

Anxiety seeps in

I feel like I'm pretending

No more norming, Fuck conforming

Reality transforming

From her to him and him to her

When pink fades to blue and blue fades to pink

And sometimes we rethink things

and I hesitate to renegade

But right now, I feel desolate

My soul is eloquently delicate and elegant

and I am transcending this

This experience has meaning

I have meaning, I have substance

Do not dismiss this.

Do not void me

Murderous Bathrooms
Caden Rocker
2016

Shot 3 times, killed.

Murdered for using the "wrong" bathroom.

What is wrong with society?

The Trans Person who was shot to death had no gun, no knife, no weapons yet no charges brought.

If someone murders me for using the "wrong" bathroom will they get away free too?

What is happening to society?

Bathroom police? Hate speech being spewed by political candidates as people cheer? Murders in the bathroom? Human beings being shot when they are not threatening anyone?

If you had to worry about being beaten, shot, or killed just for using a bathroom or walking down the street how would you find the courage, motivation, and determination to get out of bed every morning?

I Killed My Boyfriend's Girlfriend
Noah S.
2016

I killed my boyfriend's girlfriend, as she was sleeping at night.
I killed my boyfriend's girlfriend, as everything seemed all right.
The girl with the tears is now the man with the smile.
But why do I feel awful and vile?

I killed her as our lives were falling apart,
so why should you love me with all of your heart?
She was so beautiful, but oh so unhappy.
But still she made you oh so happy.

I killed my boyfriend's girlfriend. I ambushed her at night.
I killed my boyfriend's girlfriend, as he thought she was Mrs.
    Right.
Every tear I cry is for your girlfriend whom I mourn.
Every tear I cry is for your heart that I have torn.

Even though he says it's all right, it still keeps me up at night.

Fear
Noah Mendez
2016

wait until all the boys come home

always watching with

ears to wall and neck

captured in rope necklaces

lock yourself up and be quiet

even more so than the silence

the danger is yet to come and

the words have not yet died on your lips

you're worth just enough to prove a point

you are barred from all forms of relief

you are outcast even as you are invisible

rejected and labeled experiment

radioactive

failure

boy is born as good

boy dies as mistake

A Brother Found
Gavin Wyer
2012

An unknown path beckons me

Into the murky future

And compels me forward

Even in my silent fear

A guide speaks sacred words

That will not be denied

The name my soul embraces

Is brother to the men

Who stand beside me brave

And comfort my confusion

With many altered mirrors

That show me I am found

Midden
Grayson Barnes
2015

I am sometimes

smitten

by the archeology

of us

within this house.

Clinging to walls

perching on shelves and tables is

the first layer –

your mother's gift from her visit,

the decorative plates

we struggled to find

and then

hung

victoriously,

the table I kept

because it was

a way of

hurting you

yet holding on.

A layer deeper –

the poems

you returned

as if keeping them

meant keeping me,

the pictures

of places, experiences.

Your smile and face

in them assaults me.

Another layer –

troweling through the strata

for that

thing

that once existed

here

and finding it

gone,

whether by

your intent

or accident –

it doesn't matter.

I fight

to keep myself

from kicking apart

the other

artifacts.

Instead

I lay down my shovel,

climb out of

my excavation

and go look

for something new.

Perceptions
Casey O
2015

I'm sorry.
I'm so sorry.
I am so damn sorry.

I'm sorry that I am the way that I am.
I'm sorry that I am such a burden.
A confusion
An inconvenience.
To your "normal" lives.

I'm sorry,
That I have grown up.
And realized that the lies that I've been told,
are only lies.

It was a lie
the day I was born.
When they proudly stated, "it's a girl"
and gave me the pink blanket,
instead of the blue.

It was a lie
when they signed me up for the girls soccer team
and explained to me,
after countless questionings,
that I would have to be their daughter,
and never their son.

And it was a lie
when I had to check off a box under a category called "sex"
during my SAT's,

and it was a lie when I was told that I couldn't wear a tux to prom
because no matter how short I cut my hair,
I would never have a penis.

And you carry around those lies like the weight on your chest every day.
Compressing them into your body,
and into your mind.

You carry those lies around with you everywhere you go.
She.
Her.
Girl.
Young Lady.
Miss.
Mam.
Woman.

I'm looking in the mirror.
I'm seeing what the rest of this world sees, and it makes me shiver.
"boy" I say.
"girl" she says right back at me.
"MAN" I yell louder.
"WOMAN" she replies in a tone that pierces my ears.

I yell out one last time and my fist flies out to smash the reflection in front of me,
And just as her fist meets mine, the glass shatters into a million little pieces.
The lies, along with the glass fall onto the ground around me.

But they are only lies.

And I'm NOT sorry.

I am not sorry that me existing in this world is so difficult for you.
And I am not sorry that my pronouns are so uncomfortable for you.
And I am not sorry that I don't let you use my mind or my body as a psychology experiment.

"Do you have a penis" They ask.
Well that's what I like to call it.
"So you're like, a super lesbian"
I mean I'm pretty damn super, But I'm a fucking man.
"Did you have the surgery?"
As if my transition to be comfortable with myself was that simple that I could walk into a hospital without being turned away because of my gender identity that I could have some kind of magical procedure to conform to what your ideas of a "real man" are.
"So what did your parents say?"
The day I gave my mother magazine articles featuring Laverne Cox I later found them thrown into the back of my closet like some kind of fucked up metaphor.

And then there's the classic,
"So you were born into the wrong body?"
As if sex is so concrete and gendered that I have to declare that my body is wrong.
Just like they say that my identity is wrong.
Just like they say that my existence is wrong.
Because a single body part can define every essence of your being in this twisted world.
It's because of you that my body feels like a prison.
That my skin
Feels so tight that its suffocating the little bit of life that's left in me.
It's because of you that this assignment of sex to my body causes me to experience a systematic oppression cycle that's impossible to get out of like I'm stuck in an undertow.

Drowning.
 as you stand there on the sand watching and laughing.
Inviting your friends to laugh along as my lifeless body floats to
     the surface.

And the media will cover it:
"cross dresser died at the local beach"
"Dead body of a man discovered to really be a woman"
"*She* deserved it because *she* didn't conform to your gender
     norms"
When my obituary won't even use my correct pronouns
what good will dying do for me anyway?

It is because of you that I have to feel unsafe in this world.
It is because you that I have to feel unsafe in my own body.

So no, I'm not sorry.
And no,
 I was not
born into the wrong body.
I was born into a world where you have the wrong perception of
     my body.

Wrong
Para Modha
2016

I live in a world where
some would break me
with their words
with their fists
with their guns

the way I look
challenges everything they know,
shattering the foundation
of their pitiful existence

so they try to turn me into
who they want me to be

I live in a world where
some would say that
there are just two colors.
Blue and Pink.
Society tells me that
I am Pink.
I tell Society that
it is sadly mistaken

I live in a world where
strangers walk by
trapping me in a box
with their eyes
their laughter burns my ears

I fold my hands over my chest
stand up taller
hoping that they don't

mistake my biology
for who I am

I try to speak louder
shouting that I'm a boy
but they see the inconveniently shaped
jagged edges of my body
and "she" and "her" embed themselves
under my skin
again and again
I'm far too tired to dig them out

hide me in your box of expectations
poke a few holes for me to look out of
throw me into the ocean
I'm floating,
I'm breathing
but don't you dare call this living

I need to get out of here
escape to a world
where nobody defines me by
the way that I was born
where I can smash the mirror
reach across to the boy on the other side
pull him out and show him off
he is me, I am him

but I live in a world where
I'm just an Abomination
just a silly girl going through a phase
never mind how happy I feel
looking at the boy in the mirror
seeing someone beautiful for once

no matter what I do
in your eyes I'll always be

Wrong

flip the switch
try to turn me into
what you want me to be

and no matter what you do
in my eyes you'll always be
Wrong

Masculinity
Owen Paul Karcher
2016

anger.
that one is okay to show
the rest, choke down
wider distance between self
and others
less contact
breeds
more anger

Dialogue
Eugene SG Massey
2014

Despite my masculinity people still doubt my math abilities, talk down to me, whistle at me, judge my body hair

men still flirt with me they still shout at me on the street. I have yet to escape objectification. This gaze. This male fucking gaze. I apply it to myself, I help them put me down, I hide my body hair. I crave their approval of my body, my arm muscles, my haircut

Despite all the fucking gender fluidity in the world these powers, these sexist ideologies tell me I am not smart enough, attractive enough, tell me I shouldn't take up too much space, shouldn't think differently

They permeate my thoughts and my relationships to male assigned people. I recreate, through doubt and invalidation, the inequalities that I resent. Shit, I am an active participant at invalidating my voice.

"I'm not very eloquent," I always say

I have learned these powers well and internalized them

I put these men on a pedestal

Their brains. Their thoughts. Their feelings.

I raise them up. I defer to them. I respect them until I can become an upper-middle class white guy, I mold myself into one of them. I am male.

They tell me that my masculinity silences femininity that I am taking up too much space that I am dominating

My vagina is invisible to everyone. And,

I defer to these smart, eloquent upper-middle class___I let them critique. I try to change. I talk less. Take up less space.

Don't be too confident.

I defer to them. I am evaluated. They evaluate—that's what they were taught to do.

We were all taught to smoothly blend into the machine. We are self-sufficient, self-perpetuating

You can't teach someone how not to be chauvinistic

Labels
Tygh Lawrence-Clark
2015

Labels are wrong.

Labels are pointless

Labels are wrong

Labels, I hate them

How does a multiracial person in a white society know
    which box to check?
Where is the East Indian box? Does that part of me not exist?

I am black

I am white

I am blank

Labels are wrong

Labels are pointless

Labels are wrong

Labels, I hate them

I have to think about labels regarding my gender

Which box do I check?

I'm a little bit of this, and a little bit of that.

Gender fluid, gender masculine, gender female, gender queer
We are not one particular gender
We don't all fit neatly under the proverbial umbrella

Labels are wrong
Labels are pointless
Labels are wrong
Labels, I hate them

I'm not male or female
I'm human
I'm not black or white
I'm human

I'm not heterosexual, homosexual, bi-sexual, gay, lesbian or straight.
I'm not a this or a that, nor a who, which or a what.
I am a person.
I am Tygh, and I am a human being.

Labels, I hate them

Rival
Grayson Barnes
2014

We sat in your car
the street lights shining
on my clasped hands
when you
commended
my bravery
spoke of
who
you see me as now.

But now
you
cannot
love me –
women are okay
men are not.

You drew your line
and I respect that
even though I
have stumbled
so deep
into the well of you
it will take time
to clamber out.
It will still hurt less
than discovering
I have become
my own rival.

Free
Aaron Schmidt
2016

The sun fell and rose in her eyes
And she drew from the bottom of her glass a residue
Aflame the sun faltered and scorched the sides of her heart
And made home in the center
Burned away at the edges until there was more room
more empty space
An expanding hunger

And the longing pushed through her eyes
Flames of desire
Burned bright in cavernous space
Cobwebs knitted themselves in the corners
And hollow was she
When she lost the one she loved

Thread wove itself into a knot that couldn't fill the longing
And washed away with every downpour the weakened structure
As if she were trying to force tumors into her heart
But her own body disposed of her mentality
Made her forget the pieces of herself she had befriended
And lose everything in December
When snow carved its way into her lungs

And freed the holy spirit
She was released

Greeted peace and gave it absence with open arms
But as much as she'd like to believe she'd lost
She carried the heaviness of a thousand everythings on her back
Not empty
Not void
But never free

Sometimes...
Caden Rocker
2012

Sometimes I'm okay, even happy when I can quiet the constant slew of thoughts, worries, questions, doubts, fears, and feelings that swirl around in my head.
Sometimes I still wish on shooting stars.
Sometimes I wonder if I'm where I'm suppose to be in Life.
Sometimes I know I am Exactly where I am suppose to be.
Sometimes I look in the mirror and have to do a double take.
Sometimes I miss having a family of my own.
Sometimes everything can be made better by a rootbeer float and good company.
Sometimes I don't feel like I have anywhere to call Home.
Sometimes I am Proud of who I am.
Sometimes I wish I wasn't Trans.
Sometimes I could just stare at the stars for hours.
Sometimes I miss my old life.
Sometimes I wish I could just glide through life like a sting ray effortlessly swimming through the ocean.

Bird
Para Modha
2016

He was a boy.

She was a bird.

It made no difference.

He loved her.

He never flinched at her.

Not when she dyed her feathers blue

Or when she wore a suit to prom

And fake stubble.

Or when she'd borrow his boxers

And lifted her shirt to show him her binder.

Not when she asked to be called his boyfriend.

He still loved her like he'd never loved anyone before.

He loved her beak and her feathers and her talons

Yet he forgot that she was a bird.

She was a bird.

She couldn't stay on the ground.

So she flew away.

Ice Cream Grief
Eugene SG Massey
2016

I don't know exactly how it happened or when I stopped
It must've been gradual like a lightbulb that dims and flickers
    until its electric juices are sucked swallowed quenched into oblivion
And the trembling absence folds into steady omission. A tough masculinity. Into hearty never stopping. Desensitizing Into not whimpering and what can only be an attempt at freedom from the dramatic weak oversensitive in the family.
    Avoiding the discouragement of emotion the encouragement of Please Don't Cry.
It's the type of pain you swallow
One spoonful of buy-one-get-one java mint chip at a time.
You let the carton sweat and melt and get messy
You consume this stickiness before it can consume you. Licking and sucking even the dribbles off your shorts.
Cold slides over the crowns of your mouth down your throat.
    Roof sufficiently numbed lungs wheezing and heaving.
Emotions concealed just beyond
Eat enough of this ice cream that you can't quite tell if it will hurt more to stop or keep going
Freezing down into your chest into your icy cold heart
Goosebumps up and down your spine
And you think Gosh I still can't let it out. Ice cream is not fibrous. That's what roughage is for.
The kind of screaming letting out released full blood curdling throttle raw awed trauma shock to the depth of harm

Lost and Found
Dane Trotti
2016

Loss, I lost myself when I was born
AFAB
Done deal
Southern girl, frilly and compliant
Not.
Shirtless in the yard and told to go inside
Bold in the classroom and told to be more demure
Sporty, but told that girls' sports had been cancelled
Tried to wear the dress at graduation but couldn't
So I didn't go.

Loss, I lost myself when I started work
Girl jobs
Done deal
Southern men thinking it's ok to slap my ass
Not.
Picking up a keg of beer and slinging it into the cooler
Sleeping with the girls that other guys couldn't even talk to
Ostracized for being the person I was, masculine girl in a
    masculine world
Forces trying to change me
But I started going.

Loss, I lost myself in the modern work world
More girl jobs
Done deal
Growing my hair out to get the job
Not.
Not so much. I conformed, a bit
Cutting my hair off really short, wearing men's clothes

Once my 3 month's probation time was over
You can't fire me now, 'cause you know how good I am
I backed off really going.

Loss, I lost myself in relationships
Big tits
Done deal
Women liked me, men confused by me
Not.
Beginning to know myself, more man than woman
Dating women, fucking women, loving women
Loving women as a woman, as a man, as a person
Never could wrap my head around it
It's a place I have to go.

Loss, I lost myself in myself
Woman yet man
Done deal
Knowing I'm right, yet, pressure
Not.
I choose to honor that in me that is right
I change things in my body that are incongruent
I become what I always was
I am a human being worthy
of respect
This is who I am
This is where
I go.
This is where I'm found.

Still Here
Owen Paul Karcher
2016

She said I killed her sister
I looked at her,
        still here.
She is not dead.
She is me.

My loss
Johnny W. Payne
2006

You held my hand as we grew up together.
You held my hand as we laughed together.
When I changed my name; you wondered why.
Then I changed my gender; you wanted to cry.

But it's still my hand that you will not touch.
This is *my* hand that you now hate so much.
I still laugh the same, but you will not listen.
because I have a new name, and I sound different.

I don't look like the person you grew up with.
I don't look like that person, I get the gist.
But you didn't lose me, I lost a sister.
You just say I'm not me; and they call me "mister"!

Now there's only one place when I might see you again.
There are no women, and there are no men.
If we ever meet there will you know me again?
If we ever meet there will you laugh with me again?

Coming Home
Grayson Barnes
2015

When I
returned
to this place
the stultifying silence
was broken only by
my heartbeat's
solo
thud
against walls
which had once resounded with
our both
tender and terrible
words.

I drifted
from
room to
vacant
room
like a dust mote
until catatonic –
my stasis
triangulated on
bereavement, resentment, and tears.

One day I found myself
in a fugue
sweeping.

I set to work.

First
I replaced
the locks –
no one
would
ever
get
in
without
my permission
again.

Then I scrubbed away ache,
painted over anguish –
my hands
on this house
severing
the recollection
of the
heat
of yours
upon me.

Curtains
and color
became

a frontal assault
against the memories
marshalled
along the
wainscoting.

Each ring of a hammer
or slap of a brush
was a line of chant
in an incantation

for the courage to
box up what remained
of you
and
unpack
me.

An Open Letter to Little Girl
Noah Mendez
2016

you were such a pretty face
with long brown hair
natural highlights
always searching for love
in someone else's eyes
but only finding expectations
their mouths are open but all you
hear is dial tone, sirens, 911 operator

the word crazy drives you crazy
you take your mirrors and shatter them
pretend you still like yourself like this
you with your leaking eyes and open arms
you could never get enough you were
sad harmful little lost girl

i killed you off to make room for the butterfly
i don't regret your feminine blood
on these large hands

Deficit of Boyfriends
Maverick Smith
2016

Ableism
Oralism
Audism

These are the answers I could give
To questions crowding on folks' tongues

Cissexism
Kyriarchy
Cisnormativity

These are the answers I swallow
Unprepared to face the platitudes

Heterosexism
Transphobia
Heteronormativity

These are the systems of oppression
Which limit my choice of partners

Belief is in the Mind of the Beholder
Max Andeo Meyer
2014

I have no tangible proof

no quantifiable evidence

no scientific theories

tested in a psychiatry office.

I have no definite beginning

and certainly no end

at least not one that you would understand.

No words to explain why I did this.

Even if I could reveal myself

and show the incisions to you:

the money, effort, and documents,

why do I need to prove my truth?

I am who I am,

and that should be enough for you

but instead I drown in a sea

of documents, court orders, and handwritten letters

from doctors who know me no better

than you do

and I attend hearings where medical corporations

chose my fate but no one is listening

because I am of an under-served, misrepresented,

media-molested

population with no voice of our own

except in letters which will never reach

the leaders of this nation

because it is hard to speak

and be seen when your

whole goal is to be invisible.

Inappropriate Questions
Max Andeo Meyer
2014

How long have you been a man?

Since age two or ten?

Maybe starting last year when this perilous journey
    began?

No! I will always be the man that I have always been!

Do you like boys or girls?

Certainly you must be gay, they plead.

No, you dimwits, can't you see?

I like who I like.

There is a thick line between gender and sexuality.

Have you had the operation?

Which one? There are many. Why are you asking?

How would you like your genitalia to be

examined and questioned for authenticity?

Uninformed people just don't understand

It's not the surgically-modified dick that makes the man.

Do you sit or stand and where do you pee?

In the toilet just like you.

Now stop pestering me!

How do you reproduce and who would sleep with you,

all stitched and sewn and pieced together with Elmer's glue?

Well, when two people love each other very much...

Ah, forget it! Screw you!

Do your parents know? Did they react with glee?

Did you tell your employer and your Great Aunt Betty?

The idea is some will know, but others will not.

Don't make me remember what I wish I forgot!

Are you legal? May I see your ID?

Uncle Sam is coming around,

but I'm not accepted from sea to sea.

Now I ask of you please think

before you speak.

Your questions are insensitive and rude.

You have put me in quite a bad mood.

Always be polite.

Before saying ma'am or sir,

ask for preferred pronouns if you're unsure.

Never assume you know everything about me,

my trials and fears,

stuff you learned from Dr. Phil

and late-night documentaries,

but always think before you ask:

would I answer this question myself

or would I rather pass?

Troublemaker
Max Andeo Meyer
2015

Am I starting trouble?

If by starting trouble

you mean

giving a voice to the invisible,

shedding light on your mistakes,

making a place for the outcast,

then yes,

I am starting trouble.

If you find my trouble troubling,

then hell yes,

I am starting trouble.

If you find

your views widening,

your opinions changing,

your prejudices dissipating,

then yes,

I am starting trouble.

But don't tell me

I am in trouble

for troubling the system

so that you may feel
troubled.
Don't tell me
that my existence
makes you uncomfortable
when your comfort invalidates
my existence.
Get off the couch and
embrace the
dissonance.

You can't stay reclined
when the administration
is denying my rights
that you redefined
to match
your ideology.
I will not apologize
when the evidence
dispels your lies.
Only when you agree
can we compromise
that The Truth
is only a truth
and my truth

is not a heresy.

I never knew
that by speaking
my truth
I would be starting trouble.
When my mother told me
not to go to protests,
she didn't realize
I would speak loudest
in written letters
trying to justify
my existence
to the DMV, doctors, and school faculty.
If only she could understand
that by my words,
we gain collective energy
find a common core,
so we can finally
be seen
as mothers and fathers
doctors and lawyers
fully competent
thriving
human beings.

But as long as
I am viewed as trouble,
I will find
your lack of respect for diversity
troubling.

A Eulogy For Dead Names
Kai Schweizer
2016

There's a cemetery in my skull
Where the kids shed blood like milk teeth.
I watched their eyes grow vacant,
Sick with self-awareness,
Distressed and dysphoric.

They ate their anxieties
And rotted their entrails
With apathy;
Emaciated and ecstatic.

They drank themselves full of synthetic serotonin,
In stolen sips
In brown bags
In bathroom breaks
In bus backseats.

They stood stoned in Rosemount mirrors
With a mouthful of epiphanies
Licking the lids on their
Dog-eared daydreams
Of a cisgender self.
They got ashtray blues,
Goon bag blues,
Got high
And watched the streetlights levitate.

I'm tracing these broken maps in my head,
There's all these kids,
Misfits and minors,
Delinquents and dropouts,
Living in homes made of makeshift bones,

Learning self-hatred
In street corners and cubicles
In gutters and toilet bowls,
In sitcoms and romcoms and dotcoms
In forgotten prescriptions.
They learned to bury the bruises
In Sunday pews
And bourbon bottles.

They called hotlines for suicide and government,
Were dragged from ledges,
With dreams of pavement plunging,
So razorsick they saw their veins
As glowing exit signs.
They presented their wrists
To the petty politicians
And pervy priests,
Manic in their mediocrity,
Who demanded their flesh
With hatred dripping from their lips
Like an epitaph,
Empty,
And sick with ambivalence.

They died in haircuts.
They died in freeway overpasses,
They died in saltwater poems,
Were washed down stormdrains,
In the putrid Perth streets,
Beaten and bloodied in bathrooms.

I kiss their ghosts in photo frames,
In misplaced pronouns,
In splintered spines
Crumpled in coffins,
And dinner dishes.

There's a cemetery in my skull,
Where the martyrs tear themselves open.
We may never end up
In the history books,
But we fought a battle,
Sacrificed our sanity
To the cisgender sovereigns,
And we won.

Dear Homophobia and Transphobia
Jesse W.
2016

Dear homophobia,

Dear transphobia,

Your hate

Has risen suicide rates

And murder rates.

You are the reason lovers die

Without ever saying goodbye

And, "I do."

You are the reason

There are more people on the roads

Than they can hold.

You are the reason

Kids fear going to school

Because they are not protected by any rules.

You are the reason we lack basic liberties,

Such as changing facilities

And other amenities.

You are the reason

We never got the joy

Of playing with our favorite childhood toys.

You are the reason why

We are forced into clothes

That we oppose.

You are the reason why

We fear

What being queer

Will do to us.

Sincerely,

Society's scapegoat

Ps. I would advise you stop before it's too late

Sometimes My Body is a Problem
Char Utton
2016

Sometimes my chest is a parasite,
a malformed Renaissance sculpture:
two incongruous palmfuls of marble
stuck haphazard on a flat torso.

Sometimes my voice is bile in my mouth,
toe-curling, head-splitting,
pressure to be polite, demure,
a fist on my vocal chords,
tugging up an octave.

Sometimes my curves are faults on a rule,
a skeleton that does not fit:
fleshy tarpaulin draped over
an ugly lumbering automaton.

Sometimes my womb is a traitor
in an enemy camp,
hammering at the walls,
and I bleed betrayal
like Caesar torn down.

Sometimes my skin is too small,

I am an explosion in a bottle,
erupting from my cutaneous confines
until they string out like ripped jeans.

Sometimes my body is a problem
and I am Phlebas underwater.
My eulogy calls me not handsome
but pretty.

Reflection
TJ Isaacs
2016

When I was little, I was the "Apple Festival Queen".
Pretty crown of pipe cleaners,
a dress, and fancy shoes;
I was the special girl of the day.
Everyone was so proud.
I was three.
I hated myself.

I grew older, the world around me changed.
the mirror became my enemy,
and my goal was to escape from it.
No matter how many fences I jumped,
how many trees I climbed,
or how many B.B. guns I shot,
nothing could change what the world saw.
Tomboy, they would say.
I hated myself.

The mirror was a liar,
and no one cared.
I had nothing.
I had no one.
Social view of normality,
the most important thing.
My first boyfriend was handsome.
I didn't love him.
I wanted to BE him.

I wasn't.
I hated myself.

Rebellion.
Defiance.
I pretended it wasn't real.
My first girlfriend,
my first attempt to push away
from the hetero-normative life,
from the demands of society, of the mirror,
of the world that changed,
but would not let me do the same.
It was sweet, but brief.
I hated myself.

Uneven grounds,
shaking steps,
nothing could make life right for me.
My vagina was my dictator,
and it bowed to the world,
it gave into pressure,
hid behind fear.
I took one fiancé.
I took a second fiancé.
Why couldn't I be like these men?
I wanted to die.
I hated myself.

She pulled me from the wreckage,
from beneath the shards of the mirror,
that I had broken, desperate to see beyond its lies,

Desperate to be what I felt, to see what I knew.
There was no judgment, no hate,
no sense of wrongness.
Acceptance.
You are You,
words that pulled me up, dusted me off,
words that made me realize
that in a world of hate, of darkness,
a world where I was an Apple Festival Queen,
that I could bend that pipe cleaner crown
into a sword.
That I could defend the fragile self
buried somewhere under the fear,
the uncertainty,
the parts of myself that the world chose to see
instead of the parts of myself that were true.

Years have gone by.
The days and nights are long, but not lonely.
She gives me strength, cultivating my exploration of self.
Transgender.
A label, a definition,
something to help them understand.
To help ME understand.
Some hate me, even now.
But some love me, too.
Hating the self that you are not,
but loving the self that you are
Is a hard journey.
"I hate myself" is a phrase that never goes away.
The mirror is still a liar,

but it's easier to face the lies when I am not alone.

Regardless of the body that the mirror shows me,
the eyes are mine.
I can see the real me in them alone.
She can see the real me, as well.
"I hate myself"
a phrase that can't be true.
I am not the one reflected here.
When I see myself for the first time,
years down the road, perhaps,
I will tell him how much I love him.
I will tell him how happy I am to see his smile.
I will welcome him home.

Many Years Ago
Johnny W. Payne
2008

I set out on a narrow path, so many years ago.
It was a long and lonely path, that many years ago.
I walked and ran not knowing where, so many years ago.
It was a path few dared to take, many years ago.

There was a bear I had to fight so many years ago.
It stalled the plunge to be me, every year or so.
That bear made me stronger, so many years ago.
I know where I'm going now, unlike many years ago.

I finally became me, many years ago.
But there's still a shadow on my path from many years ago.
It follows me still, like those many years ago.
It's that other me that was, so many years ago.
I'll just fight that bear again, like all those years ago.
'cause life is so much sweeter now, than so many years ago.
I just wish that other me from all those years ago,
Would not interfere with me, every year or so.

Untitled
Noah Mendez
2016

made myself into something i can't understand

stuffed with silicone and glass and unused condoms

fill up my chest with manly smells and boxers

wipe off these lips paint them pale and thin

pluck off my eyelashes

lock my jaw

i am imposter

i am never enough

playing dress up in my own clothes

reeking of all these medications i take to sleep at night

The Sweater
S
2016

The sweater.
The grey and argyle one,
I love the pattern,
the touch of smooth knit wool,
like of cashmere.
The way it hangs almost just right across my shoulders,
My shoulders,
broad and soft.
The argyle sweater,
The way it rests against my curves,
the curves that refuse to dissipate,
Shrouding them into darkness,
revealed when light begins to unfetter the buttons lined upon my breast.
In that moment, anxiety begins to build,
This is not the sight I want to see.
This is not the body that I want.
My non-existent lean muscles,
The sculpt of a sagging chest.
The sweater covers it all up.
The only thing I have to deal with a dark blob of pudginess.
I can stand a little taller.
The sweater is a comfort,
Making me almost forget that I am not who I am.
My body armour,
until it comes off,
leaving me gripped with unease.
The one temporary refuge.
Encompassed within argyle threads.

Dysphoria
Oliver Robertson
2016

My body is wrong.
I look into the mirror confused.
My body has never been right to me.
It doesn't match what I have in mind.
I don't like it.
I just despise it.
My hatred for it is so strong.
I just want to cut it.
Burn it.
Destroy it.
I don't like my body at all.
I stare at my reflection with tears in my eyes.
I see body features that don't belong on me.
Why do I have these breasts?
The wrong genitals?
And a high voice?
Why do I have all these things wrong with me?
My brain is telling me everything isn't right.
What is this feeling I'm feeling?
The more it goes on I realise its dysphoria.
It makes me want to leave.
Please let me go.
It will take over me.
I want it gone before I'm gone.
Please help me from this terror inside my mind.
Rescue me from all this trouble.
I look into the mirror and truly know,
That my body has never been right and it never will be.

⌘ ⌘ ⌘ ⌘ ⌘

SECTION III

Changes

Living Authentically

Peace/Joy/Acceptance

Changes

Transition can change every part of a person's life. These changes can be subtle over many years like the physical changes from injecting testosterone or they can be abrupt like the sudden loss of an old friend.

Every transition is unique. A transmasculine person continues to make changes in his life until he feels comfortable. There is no right way to transition or a prescribed list of consecutive steps.

A transmasculine person might change his name, pronouns, legal documents, or clothing. He might take hormones to change his appearance, body structure, and voice. He might have surgery to give his body a more masculine appearance. Some people try to consciously change their mannerisms, social groups, and hobbies to match masculine stereotypes.

Apart from visible changes, transgender people change the way they view themselves. Transition can increase a person's confidence, body positivity, and outlook on life.

Some transmasculine people face unplanned life changes from their transitions like the loss of a partner, job, or family member. When so many aspects of a person's life changes, it can be difficult for loved ones to understand that the person they knew and loved will always be the same even if that person identifies at a different spot on the gender spectrum. The key parts of their personality are unchanged.

All of these changes can be terrifying. Changes make life unpredictable, but as a person journeys towards self-acceptance, their life becomes more stable than it ever was.

On the other hand, a person does not have to change anything to be masculine. If he identifies as a man, he is no less of a man if he chooses to dress femininely or if he chooses to not have surgery or to not take testosterone. His identity is defined by him. His pronouns and name are chosen by him. He is a man because he says so. Self-assertion of a gender identity is enough to identify someone as that gender. His choice to change aspects of his life is his own choice, and that choice should be respected.

Self- identifying is life altering. It gives people the power to choose how they will present themselves, how they will define themselves, and what changes they need to make to align their outward appearance with their perceived identity.

Transmasculine people can experience a lifetime of changes, growth, and self-discovery in a relatively short time span. The alterations can seem unending. Among the sea of changes, a transmasculine person's self-assertion stays constant. "I am who I am."

Living Authentically

au·then·tic
ô'THen(t)ik/
adjective; of undisputed origin; genuine.

Growing up trans, whether or not one is aware of the term, is often difficult as one tries to conform to rigid, binary gender roles. Being forced to wear dresses, playing with girls toys and being denied the opportunity to play rough and tumble with the neighbor boys is often oppressing and uncomfortable for the child.

Many realize they are "different" at an early age, sometimes well under five years old. For others, it is when they reach puberty, and the secondary sex characteristics begin to appear. Growing breasts and menstruating can be the catalyst for severe depression, anger, or rebellion. They realize their gender is not what they were told it was, and the struggles begin.

At some point, especially in recent times with it being a public topic of conversation, they become aware of the fact that there is a name for why they feel different, and they realize they are trans. From that point on, in nearly all cases, they will begin researching everything they can find on being a transgender individual. They find out about hormones and surgeries that can "fix" their bodies to match how they feel. Some begin to make plans or even immediately pursue these options, while others choose not to medically transition, but simply just "be themselves."

Once a person has gotten to this point of just "being themselves" and living in the gender they feel, with or without hormones, with or without surgery, something happens. They start feeling good about themselves. Depression lessens. Anger dissipates. And rebellion turns into dignity.

At that moment, when a trans person can look at themselves and say "Hey, I like who I am. I don't have to be or do what society expects because of my appearance. I can be me and be proud of it," it is the feeling and experience of living authentically. The feelings of peace, joy and acceptance that one feels when they get to this point are just the beginning of a new life full of discovery. One truly becomes, at that point, undisputedly genuine.

Peace, Joy, Acceptance

The goal of life is to feel peaceful, joyful, and accepted. For transmasculine individuals, those moments of happiness can be rare. There is inner and outer turmoil. Adhering your future to your past. Connecting the various lives you have lived, putting to rest the identities you have assumed. Consoling your loved ones. Assuming your rightful place in your body. Taking control of your life story. Protesting at insurance agencies. Insisting to senators that you have a right to exist, that your identity is valid, and that you belong in the bathroom which matches your gender identity. Arguing with DMV and social security workers that the government should accept your identity when it has no protocol for how to address you. Correcting and defending your name and pronouns all day because even one mishap invalidates your existence. Recognizing the injustice of those who were killed because they chose to define their gender identity. Choosing to make permanent alterations to your shell of a body against your parents' wishes. Wishing your parents well despite their hurtful words. Demanding teachers, doctors, social workers, family members, religious leaders, and presidents recognize your right to feel peace, joy, and acceptance.

When transmasculine people feel peace, joy, and acceptance, it is in a flood of love. It is someone saying they love you exactly as you are. It is feeling confident for the first time. It is the ecstasy of that first testosterone injection that you worked so hard to get. It is meeting another transgender person and feeling normal for the first time. It is hearing your chosen name for the first time. It is signing your new name for the first time. It is watching a peer defend you. It is solidarity within the trans community. It is a potluck after a day of remembrance. It is seeing your gender identity listed as an option on a form. It is placing your new license into the sleeve of your wallet.

It is the peace of feeling comfortable in your body and in your life story. It is the joy of watching your hard work come to fruition. It is the acceptance of family, friends, employers, government officials, doctors, administrators, lovers, other trans individuals, and yourself.

⌘ ⌘ ⌘ ⌘ ⌘

The men
Mitch Kellaway
2014

the men dancing
open their
hips like hasps on
dusty music boxes
twirl like wooden ballerinas
in iron times.
i, too, i know it.
the velvet whisper
of your cracked nail polish
nestled next to my ear
i wish it
worked like oil on
the joints of this
oaken body.
twirling the mainframe.
swarming through the shallow
divots.
i have to throw out
thanks that you won't
measure my heart
against this.

that it will be how
we
sit perpendicular on the couch
and i lodge the
broad of my thigh
under your feet just
so you recall in your
polished bones how I'm the
firm earth

and you are the
molten core.

and now, the men
their hands rough
with reach
grasp my arms just
where the line of hair descends.
the crook of my elbow
where the skin flaps
and the black ink,
turned gray,
wants to push out of the skin
escape with the oil
scripting lines out the follicles.
that's where you'll find
my greatest mystery.
not why i let them grasp and turn
my limb
but why i don't catch their
salt, their uneven hustle
and pressure, encode it
into the muscles and nervelines
tracing, waxing beneath
the soft perimeter.

Matter

Mitch Kellaway
2014

i get rocked. i'm rocked.
i am   rocked.
isn't this how we were always meant
to be?
won't you let me tell you a story
about that?
tights like chain link fences
your brown hair touching your brown heels
in every way
in every re-imagining i have of the day
we met.
i do it every week.
wider, with more greens and purples,
waves like heat off a
cartoon stove.
you become myth.
jaws unhinge and reach too
far backwards, tips reaching into
a sixth dimension
whenever you mean to
delicately yawn.
curl to sleep like a leopardess.
i release smooth & unbearded,
a cub in a pack with no alpha,
no beta,
no malehood, for that matter.

These Thighs
Will P. Craig
2016

These thighs

Once pried open, a cradle for another's pleasure

Once hairless, porcelain pale and smooth

Now are mine

Needle bruised, the once-hated fat of my inner thigh

Uplifted now as a target, pierced for a greater good

The whole covered now in black curling fur

Dense and lean with a man's muscle

No longer cradle to another's hips, no longer used for any pleasure but my own

These thighs, now, are mine

In this so-wrong body they are first

First to yield to the blessed T

First to transform

Never did I love this flesh

Not arm or leg or belly

Not these cursed breasts

Not the turned-up nose

But these thighs...

I stare now

And stare

And stare

What miracle is this

to see in this body

something that reflects

my self?

Geologic
Grayson Barnes
2014

A
tectonic shift
has converted
separate
islands
into a
new
continent –
the charting of which
requires
exploration.

There are
individual
interior
geographies
with
familiar
territory.

The boundaries,
however,

endure

geologic

phenomena:

convergence,

divergence,

transformation.

Such

dramatic dislocation

of these

narrow

zones

results in

sublimation,

volcanic heat,

or

tremors.

Signposts
Gavin Wyer
2011

It is still and quiet
In this place of no return
And your words are signposts
Carefully placed to show the way
Back to where I begin
Though I seek constancy
The path I tread shifts
And I am lost here
Trying to find my way
Amongst the brave men
Who walked this road
Long before I understood
That I must follow them

A Transgender Journey in Limerick Form
C.T. Whitley
2016

Body Dysphoria
This body I must flee
Watching her mirror plea
Hands touching soft rogue flesh
Insurmountable mesh
She, not the man I want to see

Coming-out
She began to disclose
Change from girl to boy clothes
An open heart
New family chart
He, now everyone knows

Surgery
His flesh is cut, sculpted and stitched
His sex is medically switched
No real pain
Relaxed brain
Anger he has left, dropped and ditched

Loss of Lesbian Community
Once this butch dyke was embraced in womanhood
Now, facial hair a barrier between them
His sisters see past him
Bittersweet this journey
Identity realized a community lost

Show me
Noah Mendez
2016

all these mirrors are shattered

and turned away

and

mirror mirror on the wall

how many more nights like this

how many more shadows to fight

I

ask you to show me a struggle

I give you a boy breaking himself

just to feel better in this skin

I give you a paradox

dipped in desperation

I'll show you someone who has

everything to lose but gambles it anyway

Masculinity on the Margins
Maverick Smith
2016

Gender is a performance
Butler boasts
What, then, does that mean
Post-transition?

Cis people grow up
Being socialized into
Gender roles & gender expressions
That match their gender identities

Trans people grow up
Identifying along a
Continuum of not cis
Not receiving the same innate socialization

And, so, post-transition, trans folks
Must determine their gender identity,
Decide how their gender expression fits
On the margin of cisnormative scripts

Artwork
Casey O.
2016

My body is a work of art

And though it is not finished yet

It is becoming more me as the seconds go by

It is constantly changing

And adjusting

And though it is not perfect

Neither am I

If I've learned anything from this journey

Its that it doesn't need to be perfect

My body is queer

And that's exactly how Its supposed to be

That's exactly how it needs to be.

Stages

Johnny W. Payne
2004

Stand a little taller, Johnny!
Hold your head up high.
Don't look down, look all around.
You're starting a new life.

Walk a little straighter, Johnny!
Carry yourself high.
Don't let them sway you. Or dissuade you.
You're living your own life.

Step a little lighter, Johnny!
Put your life on high.
Don't look back; stay on track.
You're gonna be just fine.

Live a little longer, Johnny!
Don't give up on life.
You made it through without being you,
But this time you got it right.

Look at you now, Johnny!
Look what you've become.
You've paid the price and made the sacrifice.
Now be proud of who you've become.

My Penis
Michael Eric Brown
2007

It was announced
that I was a girl.
How could I tell them
they were wrong?
My family and friends
all saw me develop
into a body
I knew wasn't me.
Putting on bras was torture
because I had to touch
those things that didn't belong.
Society said
my loving a woman
was not acceptable.
Only a man could love
a woman in that way.
But, in my mind, I always knew
I had a penis.

It was a secret
to be hidden from lovers,
for fear they would leave
if discovered, and
cautiously concealed for fear
of ridicule or harm
from discriminating scorn.
Depression and anger
became my friends, and
resentment grew for those who
put me in a box
and tried to keep me there.

Broken,
I sought to escape
and found others like me,
who had paved the way
with their own self-discoveries
to make it easier for me
to walk my own path.
I grew a beard,
and discarded the tissue
that seemed to define me
in society's eyes,

And as for my penis,
you ask, "is it real now?"
only so you can continue
to define me.
It's not up to you
to know what's in my pants
or to decide who I should love,
so why do you care?
You don't define me,
and I don't live in your box,
because it only has room for you.

The Taped and Tattered Man
Max Andeo Meyer
2014

I am a self made man
pieced together with
broken social constructs
at 1:45 in the morning
by my mother's tears.

I have a papier-mâché heart
torn and pasted,
sticking to fingers and hair,
everything except the paper
leaving a residue in the cup
of edible glue
waiting to be devoured.

All that is left in tact
is my mind
humbled by the vastness
of the universe,
yet haughty by my own
ingenuity from mastering
my identity and from
unlocking the secrets
of my galaxy
and unleashing
the beast
behind my mask,
tribal and uninhibited,

now hunted by my
former self.
My lips are sealed
to protect the future
from my past.

I am in every part
a man as real as
the one who contributed
to your life,
as complex and true
in the Frankensteinian collage
that I have constructed
under watchful eye
from stardust painted
onto tiny papers.
I recreated my fluttering
existence.

True to me
Emrys Sparks
2015

You say it's a choice I am making,
To be true to who I am,
Like I can turn it off and pretend,
That I am not a man.

Why would I choose this,
In this world full of fear?
Being trans ain't a choice,
Can I make myself clear?

Why choose to be hated,
To be treated second class,
When I could choose to be "normal,"
Act a woman and pass?

You just don't understand,
The things that I feel,
But get that it's no choice,
It's a condition, and it's real.

It turns my head against my body,
My mind against my soul,
I'm forced into a box again,
Forced into society's role.

Why would I want this,
When I could just go along,
Because pretending never helps,
You can't keep it up long.

To try would be to kill me,
The lies would destroy my heart,

I'd never tell you to lie to me,
Would never set you apart.

I could never judge a person,
Based on who and what they are,
But you feel able to do that to me,
You judge and push so far.

You don't see me as a human,
I'm certain that's the case,
'Cause if you did you might just have,
Some empathy on your face.

You talk as if you get it,
But really you do not
'Cause if you did you might,
That last awful shot.

You might stop and listen,
Just for one brief second,
To what I'm trying to tell you,
Then you'd get it I reckon.

But to you I'm other,
I'm less now I'm broken,
I'll never be worth the time,
To listen to words I've spoken.

The sad fact is were the shoe on different feet,
I'd help you and protect you,
Show you where you're safe from harm,
Where to begin again, anew.

I'm a pretty good person,
Or so I like to think,
I help my fellow humans,
Even though I'm on the brink.

So why am I treated like this,
Just for daring to be me,
For letting my self be open,
For wanting to be free.

I just want to be happy,
Is that such a crime?
Do I not deserve it,
Is this the way I serve my time?

I just want what you have,
A body matched to mind,
Sure it's hard work for me,
But I'll do the grind.

If that's what it takes,
For me to match my soul.
Then I'll take it over and over,
Cause happiness is my goal.

If I have to walk away,
From the people in my life,
Who drag me down and keep me there,
I'll cut those ties with a knife.

I'll leave and I'll choose a path,
One that suits me well,
Cause in this darkness,
I can no longer dwell.

The Catharsis Condition
I.A. Avery
2016

"I am not this hair, I am not this skin, I am the soul that lives within"~ Rumi

When I look in the mirror, who exactly do I see? My mind keeps racing...
After I have changed my body
After surgery
Will you still love me?
I bite my lip, because I know with each coming year I will change inevitably
What if I don't believe in defining myself by a binary?
Will you still respect me?

Who should I choose to be? The question I had been asking myself unapologetically
To know that you have finally been given the chance to unfold, like a flower nourished by the sun
Like the weary pilgrim delighted in finding his destination, so he can then be at peace with himself
This life we are given, we only have one
So I decided I would do the best I could, I would embrace the journey
Still my curiosity implored me
Would you support me?

Staring at my appearance I now ask aloud "Who am I?"
I pause to roll my shirt up over my chest and in the mirror scars stare back
Are they cruel or are they kind? The truth is... they are mine
It is then I decide that I will wear ALL my scars with pride
Beyond the harsh gender scale, the question of whether I am truly male or female; persists yet another question...

Do I have the strength to live, to love and to feel?
I took some time and let it soak in; The answer was yes and for that cause I decided I would be strong

A note to all those that wish to travel with me on my journey; you must know that true love transcends beyond soul and body
To everyone who is curious as to why we go through all the pain; my answer to you is simple
We are humans
We are passionate, we are authentic but I assure you we are not insane!
Nor clothes, cash or cars can define who we are
For us we are souls transformed to highest part of our being
We will seek to find harmony with others, because if you wish to heal you cannot conceal who you are Be proud my friends that you have come so far

I let my shirt fall to the floor and smile as I realize I can finally be at peace with who I am
So it is with this last bit of knowledge I impart to you
Know that people will come and go, I decided that if you leave I will realize it was not meant to be
But if you stay, you will be the sunshine that I so need to brighten my day
So Thank You, you are truly beautiful indeed

To all those who dare to dream beyond what you are told, go seek out opportunities and be bold!
Know that true happiness comes only from the soul

Conglomeration of Genders
Shaun B.
2015

Amalgamated emotions flow through me

Conglomeration of genders

I am aberrant of social expectations

Deviant in my design

I stain the window panes

Tell me

Does the rainbow come in neutral?

Is my pudenda pink or purple?

Gift wrapped in pecan brown.

My protoplasm suffocates

Enlarged atoms press down upon my chest

Incipient embryos crush my back with a thousand would be, could be's

Tell me

Does the rainbow come in neutral?

Because the multiplicity of colors will not stain my window panes

They deviate from social expectations

Conglomeration of gender

Amalgamated emotions flow through me.

Am I sexy?
Al Cusack
2015

Am I sexy?
Can someone who looks like a 12 year old boy be sexy?
(But since I got a haircut I am pushing 15!)
Can someone with the chubby face of a baby
The hint of a beard I'll grow someday (maybe)
And the swooping hips of a full grown lady
Be sexy?
Can the mix match mess of a queer person's body
Be sexy?
Can I be sexy to anybody
When I see my body
Is a jigsaw puzzle with miss matched pieces
Making do with last minute changes so the value decreases?
I've got thighs as wide as old trees
I wear my brother's old tees
He probably wore this t-shirt in middle school
Sometimes I think I'd make a beautiful woman
If I had taken a moment
To realize my body's more suited
To that social institution
Can I be sexy
When I've been too busy trying to accept myself
And not learning how to love myself?
Too worried about finding somewhere safe to pee
To have the luxury of wondering if somebody loves me?
Can I be sexy
When the body I'm in
Is the body of someone stuck
In a social experiment
Not the body of someone who's worth
The eyes that are looking?
Can I be sexy?

Yes I can
And yes I am
I am sexy
Because
I have a spirit hotter than my flaming hair
And self-respect that runs deeper than my ocean eyes
I am sexy
Because
I may look fifteen
But I am the most beautiful fifteen year old looking queer
    you've ever seen
I have curves as smooth as satin
Strong legs with tiger pelt hair
And I dare you to find a pair of pants my butt don't look great
    in!
I am sexy
Because
Once I stopped looking to society
For what I ought to be
I found that no one looks better looking like me
I am confident
I am gorgeous
I am passionate
I am full of care and empathy
I am youthful
I am joyful
And, oh man, am I sexy!

One Instant
Grayson Barnes
2015

One instant you're talking.

With a deep breath you sleep,

wrist draped across my cheek,

fingers in my hair,

your palm domed

over my ear.

I hear

the ocean.

Birthrite
Gavin Wyer
2013

Is this my birthrite
to stand with these men
whose sacred brotherhood
goes across time and space
to the very beginning of G-d
and whose unrelenting pain
scars the souls of all men?

Is their truth also mine
in a final deception revealed
and long awaited homecoming
beckoning from generations lost?

Is my final name revealed
to be known at last as one
and claim this heady burden
of title drenched in blood
to join this endless chain
of unbroken family pride
that comes at such a cost
and gives no quarter?

Is this the secret knowledge
tattooed upon my soul
that my bone and blood and skin
remember still in quiet places
where G-d awaits discovery?

Does this thing lay claim to me
While I yet with hesitance
Explore forbidden texts
Only to find name unspoken
Resides within the seeking?

Breakthrough
Michael Eric Brown
2012

Thoughts of youth
powerlessness,
confusion,
endless questions.

The want of
comfort,
congruence,
something more.

Years of compliance, because
it was what it was, but
it was not me,
it was another.

Nameless dissonance held me
deep in the grip of "normal."
Society
told me it should be.

An acceptance, suddenly,
a vulnerability.
Understanding
it was meant to be.

Defying society,

emanation of true self,
transformation,
unearthing of me.

Thoughts of now,
reality,
certainty,
no more questions.

Haunted By Myself
Emrys Fevre
2016

I remember you,

often unexpectedly.

You surprise me

and remind me,

of times I've chosen to forget.

You whisper in my ear.

[**Author note:** This poem was written as a monthly writers group challenge to write a poem starting with the words "I remember." Early on in my transition (a couple of decades ago) I tried to not remember my (female) past but, as I've gotten older I've made peace with that other self]

Forthright
Max Andeo Meyer
2014

If I told you the truth,
would you still speak to me

in a manner of reverence,
or would I be a blight

on your perfectly-formed society
in which some people

aren't made perfectly
and must take matters

into their own hands
to fix what you say

should have been made perfect
in the first place?

⌘ ⌘ ⌘ ⌘ ⌘

CONTRIBUTORS

I.A. Avery, also known as Rev. Ian Avery, was born an Intersex individual and had a life changing "female to male" transition between the years of 2010-2015. As an author, he is prominent in both the Spiritual and LGBTQI communities. Familiar with the struggle all Transgender and Intersex people face, he is also passionate about human rights and encourages everyone to have compassion and be true to themselves. It is his hope that one day America will break down its gender binary and realize that at our core we are all human.

Shaun B. began socially transitioning when he was 10, then medically at 16. Shaun is asexual and more gender neutral, and because of this, doesn't feel like any identity fits. Shaun is just kind of floating somewhere undefined. Shaun wrote a poem out of fear of regret, asking himself "If I have surgery now will I regret it at 75? What about the children I could've had? What if I retransition, will I regret not fully transitioning?" At the same time, he has been living as male for so long that he can't even imagine what it would be like being female, but yet he's not fully male.

Isaac Oscar Bainbridge was born in England in September of 2001. Now, in May of 2016, he lives openly as a pansexual, transgender male. After coming out to his mum in the summer of 2015, his gender identity was brushed aside until a few months later when his identity became more accepted by close family members and friends. Since receiving support from friends and family he has helped his school make critical steps towards supporting LGBT students and plans on continuing to do so during his time there. Isaac enjoys creative subjects, such as art and design, so started writing some slam poems after watching videos on the internet. Now he wants to get his work out there, especially to educate others on the struggles that Transgender individuals face on a daily basis.

Grayson Barnes teaches Humanities and Fine Arts at Butler Community College in Andover, KS. His writing is more often devoted to creating instructors' manuals and writing for LGBTQ publications, although his first love is, and always will be, poetry. He currently lives in Wichita, KS with the sweetest dog in the world and a bevy of cats.

Michael Eric Brown is known for his contributions both on and offline, especially in the realm of social justice and gender concerns. A scholar who is interested in how people's thoughts, feelings, and behaviors are influenced by the actual, imagined, or implied presence of others, Michael is working his way towards a PhD in Social Psychology in order to educate society and provide needed research on the lives of transmasculine individuals. Michael is the author of *Pencil Me In: A Trans Perspective in a Gendered World* (Boundless Endeavors 2015) and *A Herstory of Transmasculine Identities: An Annotated Anthology* (Boundless Endeavors 2016).

Will P. Craig is a queer 30-something trans man from Houston, Texas, who spends his time writing novels, reading anything and everything, and watching as much bad sci-fi as he can get his hands on. Under the pen name Thursday Euclid, Will has published a number of Rainbow Award-winning queer romance novels. Under his own name, he plans to publish trans-focused YA stories. At the end of 2015, he started his medical transition with the full support of his two amazing teenagers and looks forward to the day others are as accepting of his identity as they are.

Al Cusack is a student at St. Thomas University. They are a nerd and therefore are seeking degrees from three departments: Sociology, Human Rights, and Communications and Public Policy. Al has no hobbies or interests because they keep busy with organizing and planning events for queer and trans people.

Al has little confidence in their poetry but hopes you will enjoy their piece.

Emrys Fevre is a mostly nocturnal individual who spends his nights writing, reading and enjoying the lack of competition while grocery shopping at 3 AM. He enjoys loud heavy metal, collects skulls and his favorite color is black (until they invent a darker color). Yellow sports cars, trucks and motorcycles make him angry. He lives with his boyfriend, his 19 yr old son, two dogs, a potentially psychotic parrot, an angry iguana and three cats. He's allergic to cats. The cats love him. Cats are jerks.

Joshua Daniel Hunt is a 47 year old transgender male who transitioned 16 years ago. He is now a political activist and gender identity education trainer in the state of VA. Josh battled dysphoria from the age of 5 and was suffocated into a person he was not aware he was biologically. Mr. Hunt also does research in transgender issues and is currently working on social transitioning in transgender youth.

TJ Isaacs is a writer/artist living in California, USA. Currently making a living working night security, they write and craft in their off-hours, hoping to finish their first trilogy soon. When they are not busy working, writing, or crafting, they are spending time with their family and friends, including their two cats, Dorian and Widget. They have won several official awards for their sculptures, mostly in Modesto, California, as well as a handful of unofficial awards for writing blurbs and short stories online. They have been to 46 US states, and five Canadian provinces, and hope to continue to travel in the future!

Owen Paul Karcher is a transmasculine art therapist and social justice consultant based in Madison, WI. Owen works through the creative process in groups and with individuals to deepen personal understanding, growth, connection, and healing. Owen believes in the healing power of art and creativity to bring about personal and collective liberation. They have mostly written nonfiction articles, and have come back to poetry as a somewhat unfamiliar medium. Their primary artistic expression has been with clay, paint, and wood in recent years. If you want to learn more about what Owen is up to, check out their website at: www.arttherapymadison.com

Mitch Kellaway is a biracial queer trans man who works as a writer and editor. He is the editor of two collections of non-fiction writing by trans men: *Boys Do Cry* (on violence) and *Manning Up* (on self-realization; co-edited with Zander Keig). His writing has appeared in *The Advocate, Lambda Literary Review, Original Plumbing, Mic, Mashable, The Huffington Post*, and *Everyday Feminism*. Reach him at MitchKellaway.com.

Tygh Lawrence-Clarke is a 51 year old transman. He was born in Beverly Hills, CA and was raised by a single mother, who was a prominent physician. His family moved to Las Vegas when he was 11, where he remained for most of his life. He retired in 2011 from the pharmacy field to become a stay-at-home Dad. He now lives in the woods of New Hampshire with his wife, son and his menagerie of pets. Since his transition, Tygh now spends his free time advocating for the transgender community. He has a YouTube channel where he documents his transition and makes educational videos. He, with the help of his wife, is also working with a nonprofit organization called *41%*, which strives to pair people in the transgender community with supportive volunteer peers in an effort to address the suicide problem. Despite the challenges Tygh faces every day, he couldn't be happier now that he is living his life as his true self.

Eugene SG Massey graduated from Wesleyan University as an anthropology major in 2015 with a capstone titled "Leaving the Nest: Life at the Neoliberal University." Since graduating, they have worked at a domestic violence crisis center, assisted with research around domestic violence, interned at the Massachusetts Museum of Contemporary Art (MASS MoCA), and currently manage a DIY Bike Collective in Boston.

Noah Mendez is a 17-year-old trans man who is just starting out in the poetry world, but hopes to produce writing that means something to all of you. He was an Urban Word Contest Finalist, has been published in the *Rising Phoenix Review, Brouhaha Magazine, Thank You For Swallowing*, and has a writing blog over at emergincy.tumblr.com He likes to write in a style that he would call experimental mixed with Beat poetry and a dash of e.e.cummings.

Max Andeo Meyer is studying agricultural education at New Mexico State University. He hopes to use his writing to educate people about sustainable agriculture. Max has used writing to express himself and educate people since the age of three. He likes sharing his perspective of the world through his poetry at open mic nights. Max helped create the first transgender student organization at his university. He is passionate about LGBT and sustainable agriculture activism.

Para Modha is a seventeen-year-old transmasculine and gender non-conforming writer, poet, and high school student. He enjoys music, reading, theatre, volunteering, and defying societal expectations about gender. Para considers his queerness to be a significant aspect of his identity. He writes poetry as a form of self-expression about his own life and the struggles of being a South Asian, transgender young adult. Para is passionate about human rights, particularly issues concerning the queer community and racial minorities.

Kaleb Morrison is queer, genderqueer and quite short. They enjoy sweaty dance parties, carrying heavy things, direct action resistance, and cookies. They spend most of their time staring, open mouthed, at the mountains and waters of St'at'imc and Coast Salish territories. Kaleb is involved in land defense, food security and public art. You can find their work at kstonebc.ca and in the backyards of East Vancouver.

Casey O. is a twenty year old transgender man who uses poetry as way of self-expression as well as a way to advocate for trans rights and educate the community. He believes that poetry is a powerful way of creating self-acceptance. He first went to poetry as a way to cope with dysphoria and rejection when he was first coming out as transgender at the age of sixteen. He now writes and performs spoken word as a way to educate the community on what it means to be transgender by sharing his own story through poems. He hopes that more trans youth will find poetry as a healthy coping mechanism and path to self-acceptance.

Johnny W. Payne is a 56 year old military veteran who started full female-to-male (FTM) transition at age 43. Married to his wife, Maggie, of 10 years, they are raising their 4 year old granddaughter while he is working on a Bachelor's degree hoping to land a career in counseling. He and his wife voluntarily mentor individuals and couples starting their own transition. Although his daughter, son-in-law, and grandchild, as well as Maggie's children, support and accept him as he is, Johnny's birth family has rejected and alienated him for no other reason than his transition to male. Johnny is an artist in pen and ink and in stone carving. His wife, also an artist, works in mixed media painting. Johnny, Maggie, and their granddaughter enjoy camping, music, and the arts. They live in North Carolina with two parrots, two cats, and a dog, all rescued animals.

Marval A Rex is the professional name of Marval Angela Rechsteiner. He is a self-proclaimed mutant, artist and Jedi apprentice to the Master we call Life. Although he primarily identifies as a ceramicist, Marval is open to any and all mediums in expressing his indomitable spirit. His most recent artistic forays include video art and the photographic memoir of his gender adventure. For the sanctity of his mental and emotional health, Marval lives Life as Art, which means he believes that every moment is a moment full of intentional wonder and hidden masterpiece. Alongside his surrender to his inner muse (boy is she sassy), Marval holds a deep sense of spirituality, moving beyond any existential angst to find magic in all things. His daily meditative practice includes throwing a hexagram for the *I Ching* or *Book of Changes*, consulting astrological transits, and imbibing the wisdom of *Gene Keys* and Human Design. Marval's artistic website can be found at kinglyvisions.jigsy.com, his artist Facebook at facebook.com/marvelartking, and blog at kingly visions.blogspot.com.

Oliver Robertson (Oli for short) is a transman/non-binary pansexual/panromantic. They are from Melbourne, Australia and is in year 11 (2nd last year of high school). They came out as transgender to their school (which is an "all" girls school) in 2014. Later this year, they will be starting hormone replacement therapy. They have become more confident in themselves over the past 2-4 years with the acceptance of their gender identity and orientation.

Caden Rocker identifies as an FTM/Non-Binary/Trans Human and is currently 32 years of age. They spent the majority of their childhood in a small town in Upstate New York and began to discover their true gender identity at the age of 22, after moving away from their hometown. Caden currently lives in Albuquerque, New Mexico where they are an active member in the activist community and do work with non-profit organizations that help the LGBT community especially LGBT Youth. The experience of finally being able to have Top Surgery in 2015 after waiting for numerous years has had a profound experience on Caden and only furthered their commitment to create change in whatever ways possible. In addition to writing Caden enjoys spending their spare time outdoors in nature, taking pictures, or spending time with their dog, Cooper.

Felix J Ross is the graphic artist who designed the main cover graphic. Felix is an FTM transgender individual. Felix doesn't necessarily believe in the fine line of "masculinity" and "femininity." Instead, Felix believe in the empowerment of self-expression. The way Felix chooses to express true self is by wearing a lot of bright colors (such as pinks and pastels) while occasionally sporting an oversized jean jacket and cap. Felix is an LGBTQA+ activist from Texas and currently studying animation at New Mexico State University.

S - Coming from a traditional Nepali background and as a Third Culture Kid growing up traveling the world, S took a while to understand their queerness. They like to say that they are a more "masculine-energy-based" person with feminine traits. Their peers like to describe them as genuine, sincere and fun person. S loves stories and believes there is nothing better than listening to stories of yore. Other interests include anything and everything on drama and theatrics, history, and listening to nature. They also like poetry and fresh apple pie.

Noah S. is a 18 year old guy from Copenhagen, Denmark who dreams about going to university. He got into poetry through his friends who liked to perform their poems. When he was 14 years old, he discovered that he was trans, but at that time he was so unsure of himself that he didn't come out. Then he met his boyfriend and he forgot everything about him being trans until three years later. When he was 17, he rediscovered that he was trans, and a few month later he came out. He is unsure about HRT and surgeries, so now he just takes life one step at a time.

Aaron Schmidt began writing at the age of twelve, ambition derived from iconic admiration of a certain acclaimed author who wrote a few stories about a boy-wizard. However, with the encouragement of a good friend, Aaron instead became enthralled by the simple, yet emotionally captivating forms of slam and free-form poetry. Together with their best friend, they started a "Poetry Club" at their high school, where writing helped them a lot in the coming out process, and in living their life as a Queer person in general.

Kai Schweizer lives in Perth, Australia; the most isolated capitol city in the world. He's part of the new breed of emerging poets in

Perth who tackle issues of identity, body, sex and place within culture and society with an unashamed in-your-face confessional style.

Liam Smietanski is a Graduate Student in Art. He has been a Renaissance Man of the Arts all his life: drawing, sculpting, and writing, to name a few. Although Liam has written many short stories and poems, this is the first time his work will be on display to the public. Liam is in his 4th year of transition and has felt very blessed that his family and friends have loved him along the way. He also has been mentoring other trans men just staring their journey.

Maverick Smith has always been interested in social justice and equity. A published poet, writer and the editor of a youth anthology, Maverick explores the themes of social justice and equity in their work. A deaf*, queer, trans*, dis/abled, genderqueer settler, Maverick currently resides on the traditional lands of the Mississaugas of the New Credit where they are engaged in community work related to the intersectionality of their various identities.

Emrys Sparks is a recently out trans man living in the UK. He is a student and writes poetry as a way to vent emotional stresses and to try and allow others to empathize. The way people dismiss and belittle trans people is a real annoyance for him and he has no time for bigots in his life. Stubborn and determined are two words often used by his close friends to describe him.

Dane Trotti successfully escaped from the Bible belt and now lives in New England with their awesomely supportive wife and an ornery but loveable pooch. They love going to musical theatre in NYC and frequenting museums whenever possible. Dane has worked for over a decade as an electronic resources support specialist for a large academic research library. Absolute heaven for a bibliophile! Dane sees more travel and much blogging in their future!

Char Utton is a student from the UK who has recently completed a BA in Graphic Design and is now looking to expand their skillset and collect as many experiences as they can. They are an avid reader of all genres, and their other hobbies include rollerblading and languages. They have had a passion for writing since childhood, and have experiences with poetry, original fiction and fanfiction. Char has been previously published in Young Writers' *Talkin' 'Bout My Generation - West Country*, and they are in the early stages of writing a book to introduce young children to gender-neutral pronouns.

Jesse W. is a trans male who enjoys spending his time writing, filming, taking pictures, and playing hockey. When Jesse is not absorbed in taking part in his passions, he is spending time with his friends, family, or his beloved cat. Right now, Jesse is attending high school in the United States, where he hopes to get his diploma. Most importantly, Jesse enjoys utilizing his time to write about himself in third person.

Joshua "Tygerwolfe" Ward is a transman in his thirties. An accomplished writer and artist, boasting many articles on his website, Tygerwolfe.com, as well as an article in the upcoming trans-focused pagan publication *Arcane Perfection*, and a children's book published under his birth name, currently in rewrites.

C.T. Whitley is the co-editor of *Trans-Kin: A Guide for Family and Friends of Transgender People* (Boulder Press 2013), which won a 2013 International Book Award. His work has also been featured in such publications as Manning Up (Transgress Press 2014), *Letters for My Brothers* (Wilgefortis Press 2011), and *Gender Outlaws* (Seal Press 2010). He holds an M.A. from Michigan State University and is working on completing a Ph.D. in Sociology. Visit him at www.cameronwhitley.weebly.com.

Howie Wielandt is a writer in the process of finishing three books, and lives on Whidbey Island. After working at Walmart, he learned: "I'd rather be a starving artist than have my value as a person be based upon how fast I scan items on a conveyor belt." He hung up his vest and exchanged it for his true love, writing. When not having stare downs with computer screens, he's watching YouTube, cooking or researching cures for writer's block. At sixteen Howie came out as trans and has fought every step of the way to begin transitioning, and for the rights of trans people. His goal is to educate and prevent ignorance; that being the cause of violent attacks on trans people. He's raising money to pay for top surgery and is working on a fiction called "Transformer" a story about a homeless teen. You can reach him on Tumblr @fabulous-by-choice.

Dexter J Wiseman is a 48 year old transman, who has known since the age of 5 or 6 that he didn't feel female, but for many years did not realize that he could do anything to change that. he has been out to friends and family for almost 2 years and socially transitioned and living full time as a man for 12 months still waiting to start medical transition. He has been very lucky to have fantastic support from friends, family and colleagues alike, and feels humbled and grateful for this.

Gavin Wyer is a 57 year old trans man who transitioned late in life at 52. When he transitioned he also left his career and home to begin a new life as a man. He has published in two anthologies and has online videos talking about his experiences. His goal is to become a mentor and foster parent to trans identified youth.

⌘ ⌘ ⌘ ⌘ ⌘

REFERENCES

Brown, M.E. (2015). *Pencil Me In: A Trans Perspective in a Gendered World*. Miami, FL: Boundless Endeavors, Inc.

Clements-Nolle, K. Marx, R. and Katz, R. (2006). "Attempted Suicide Among Transgender Persons: The Influence of Gender-based Discrimination and Victimization." *Journal of Homosexuality. 51*(3). 53–69

Cohen, Jacqueline N. & Alderson, Kevin G. (2014). "'Psychology Works' Fact Sheet: Gender Dysphoria in Adolescents and Adults."

Gay and Lesbian Alliance Against Defamation. (2013). "End Healthcare Discrimination for Transgender People."

Grant, J.M., Mottet, L.A. & Tanis, J. (2009). *Executive Summary. Injustice at every turn: A report of the national transgender discrimination survey*. National Gay and Lesbian Task Force and the National Center for Transgender Equality.

National Center for Transgender Equality. (2016). "Map: State Health Insurance Rules."

Prince, V. (2005). Sex vs. gender. *International Journal of Transgenderism, 8*(4), 29–32. (Original work published 1973).

www.ingramcontent.com/pod-product-compliance
Lightning Source LLC
LaVergne TN
LVHW051521070426
835507LV00023B/3231